Liverpool Tramw

Volume 1 – 1869 to 1932

Richard Buckley

This lively view of Lime Street shows how people got around in late Victorian towns. On the right is a fairly typical horse bus of the type used on city services. It has small front wheels, would be hauled by a pair of horses and has a flimsy ladder to reach the top deck. To the left are trams on the Bootle route pulling into and out of their terminus at the Quadrant. Alongside the kerb are horse cabs. Other trams are passing St. George's Plateau, with its equestrian statues of the young Prince Albert and Queen Victoria; between them stands Disraeli, erected in 1883. Behind the Wellington Column at the top is the pillared late Victorian County Sessions House. The cluster of older commercial premises reveals a different Liverpool to the 'show' buildings.

Text © Richard Buckley, 2014.
First published in the United Kingdom, 2014,
by Stenlake Publishing Ltd.
54-58 Mill Square,
Catrine, KA5 6RD

Telephone: 01290 551122
www.stenlake.co.uk

ISBN 9781840336610

**The publishers regret that they cannot supply
copies of any pictures featured in this book.**

Acknowledgements

This book shows how tramways in Liverpool developed from the days of horse-drawn vehicles to the early 1930s. It includes a fairly comprehensive record of the different vehicles used, set against the background of the city they served. It is not a history in depth. For that the reader should turn to the magisterial five volume history of public transport in the city by J. B. Horne and T. B. Maund. Various people have assisted with the author's other deficiency, that of not being a Scouser. Martin Jenkins has offered helpful advice in this direction. Other books, cited below, have also been referred to, very often in order to glean details from their photographic coverage. The Pevsner Guides are always invaluable in describing the fabric of a city. I am, as always, grateful to Roger Smith for drawing the maps. Proof-reading was carried out by Pat Malham and the late Bruce Maund; the latter, one of the two authors cited above, also saved me from a number of factual errors. Full responsibility remains the author's however.

I have received the utmost generosity from many people who have shared photographs and opened their archives to me. Peter Bloxam's collection of picture postcards is a priceless resource. So are the carefully annotated photographs provided by the late Norman Kellett and the collection amassed by Peter Carr. Other people who have supplied illustrations include Alan Brotchie, Ted Gray and Arthur Kirby, all of them loaning items from their collections entirely free of charge. It has also been useful to draw on David Packer's resources. This book could not have been written without their help. Because the pictures came largely from collections and were often copies from the original, it has by no means always been possible to identify the photographer by name. Some were supplied many years ago by (the former) Liverpool City Transport. Individuals whose work is definitely represented include D. Conrad, H. G. Dibdin, F. Mussett and G. N. Southerden. Although my mother's family home was in Walton and I used to visit there as a child, only three later photographs are my own. Given the family connection, however, it has been a pleasure to explore long-buried memories of Liverpool and of its fine tramway.

This volume covers the history from the early years of horse traction through to approximately 1932, a time when Liverpool's electric trams had reached what was, for most other tramway systems, the high water mark of development. Would the city's develop further, or would they decline? Volume 2, in the course of preparation, will illustrate what happened next.

Further Reading

Chandler G., *Victorian and Edwardian Liverpool and the North West from old photographs*, B. T. Batsford Ltd, 1972

Gahan J. W., *Seventeen Stations to Dingle: the Liverpool Overhead Railway remembered*, Counryvise Ltd & Avon Anglia Publications, 1982

Horne J. B. & Maund T. B., *Liverpool Transport, Vol. 1: 1830-1900; Vol. 2: 1900-1930; Vol. 3: 1931-1939; Vol. 4: 1939-1957; Vol. 5: 1957-1986* [volume 5 relates only to bus services], LRTA & Transport Publishing Company, published respectively in 1975, 1982, 1987, 1989 & 1991.

Rothwell C., *Britain in Old Photographs: Liverpool*, Book Clearance Centre & Budding Books, 2001

Sharples J., *Liverpool* (Pevsner Architectural Guides series), Yale University Press, 2004

Introduction

Liverpool grew up on a narrow peninsula between the river and a tidal inlet, known as the Pool. Its maritime roots run deep. Some of the first settlers in the area were Norsemen, the name of one of them perhaps being corrupted to form 'Liver'. Another explanation is 'lifer' meaning muddy. Birds don't come into it! The township first became important in the reign of King John who needed a safe anchorage for his fleet so he could launch an attempt to crush a rebellion in Ireland. He made Liverpool a borough in 1206. His emblem was an eagle, which probably accounts for the city's symbol being avian – a sadly pedestrian explanation for the famous Liver birds. A castle was built and a town laid out, but no trace of either remains except for the 'H' shape of the medieval streets. Towards the end of the middle ages the castle came into the hands of the Molyneux family and, at about the same time, the Stanleys, who were local notables, were created Earls of Derby (named after the local township of West Derby, not the county town in the Midlands). Both families continued to play a role in Liverpool's development for many hundreds of years.

By the Tudor period the port had evolved into a commercial one, a process assisted during the 17th century by the silting up of the Dee, meaning that Liverpool took over the Irish import/export trade from Chester. The city enjoyed immense prosperity during the next century as a result of the triangular trade between Britain, Africa and the Americas, on the second leg of which the cargo was slaves. No less than sixteen lord mayors owed their prosperity to this traffic. However once it was abolished in 1807 the connections already formed helped to maintain the wealth of the city's merchants through, for example, the cotton trade and sugar refining. Some of their fine town houses survive from this period.

The Pool itself was inadequate for a growing port and the first enclosed dock opened to shipping in 1715, to which four more were added by the close of the century. No other city had more than one. In 1783 there were roughly 200 Liverpool-registered ships; less than two decades later it was more like 1,000. To remain a successful entrepot, however, the city needed good inland communications. The first turnpike roads were constructed in the mid-18th century and in the years up to 1816 local rivers were made navigable and new canals cut. The world's first railway in the modern sense was opened to Manchester in 1830 and, before long, railways would link Liverpool to the entire country.

In 1839 Cunard secured the mail contract for the Transatlantic crossing to North America, making the city the equivalent of today's Heathrow Airport. Later rivals included the White Star Line (with which Cunard later amalgamated) and the Inman Line, which carried the US mail and, later, gained a part-share in the GPO contract too. Inman's had started out with services to Philadelphia, as opposed to New York, but later transferred to the latter. Financial difficulties in the early 1890s led to its takeover by the American Line. Many new docks were opened and in 1857 the port was enlarged to include both banks of the Mersey, it being administered by a new Mersey Docks & Harbour Board. Other industries, such as pottery, flour milling and match making, developed. The population grew rapidly (partly due to boundary enlargements) from 78,000 in 1801 to 286,000 in 1851. Such a large conglomeration of people, added to by a daily flow of passengers by rail, Transatlantic ship and, not to be forgotten, the Mersey ferries, required some form of local transport to move around the burgeoning city.

During the 1830s horse buses were introduced to most areas, but they were small, rode roughly and cost too much for all except the middle classes. Tramways had meanwhile been developed in the USA using larger vehicles on smooth rails which could therefore carry more passengers at lower fares. Merseyside played an important role in the early introduction of this American concept to Britain, though the first development was in fact home-grown. Running behind the docks along the Liverpool bank of the Mersey were railway lines to carry freight to and from the ships. William Joseph Curtis designed a 'railway omnibus' with moveable wheels so it could run either on the road or on rails, giving it the ability to move off the track when a train approached. In 1859 he obtained permission to operate this on the docks railway and it ran successfully for a month or more. Local bus proprietors later took over the idea and ran a similar service until the early 1870s. Meanwhile, across the Mersey in Birkenhead, the (nearly!) appropriately named American entrepreneur George Francis Train opened the UK's first genuine street tramway line on 30th August 1860. The trams ran on a sort of metal plate with a ridge to keep them in place. The vehicles were a great improvement but the rails were quickly deemed a nuisance to other road users and had to be replaced with grooved rail, similar to that used today in central Manchester (most other lines Train built elsewhere were simply closed).

In Liverpool two brothers, William and Daniel Busby, had run horse buses since 1834 and, on 22nd July 1861, they opened a short tram route (perhaps also suitable for use by their steel-tyred buses) at Old Swan, then outside the city boundary. It used a version of Train's plateway, but though improved it was still deemed an inconvenience and was removed during 1862. Six years later the Liverpool Tramways Company was formed by Act of Parliament with authority to build a city circle and two branches, to Dingle and to Walton. The first two lines were opened on 1st November 1869. The Walton branch was added in 1870 but further extensions were difficult to achieve because of opposition from both the council and the bus concerns.

These impediments were overcome by a merger between the Tramways Company and a Busby-owned bus company in 1876 to form the Liverpool United Tramways & Omnibus Company and also by the council taking over the tracks and building new ones, which the company had to lease back. Also, the need for specific legislation had been removed by the passage of the 1870 Tramways Act, which provided general powers (with strict limitations) to construct new lines. By 1885 there were 60.75 miles of tramway (not all in use, as the council had built some lines speculatively which the company did not want to use), 2,894 horses, 207 trams and 272 buses, the whole providing a rewarding investment to shareholders and a valuable service to the public.

Horse trams were, however, expensive to run and, as the 19th century drew to a close, increasingly anachronistic. Various alternatives were tried, the most satisfactory (though dirty) for UK operators being steam trams. The only passenger-carrying experiment in Liverpool, however, involved a compressed air locomotive designed by Colonel Beaumont and, though it worked tolerably well, the idea was not taken up. Railed electric traction had been proven technically since the late 1870s but the difficulty was how to feed the current safely to moving vehicles. Britain's first true electric tramway opened in Blackpool in 1885 using an underground electrified channel known as a conduit; much altered, the line is still running today. Overhead wires were more attractive to promoters, though, because they would be cheaper and less prone to breakdown, but no foolproof method of conducting current from wire to vehicle yet existed. Once the trolley pole, a sprung collecting arm, had been developed in the USA this became the system of choice. The United Company then applied for powers to run electric trams but, meanwhile, the whole undertaking was transferred to Liverpool Corporation from 1st January 1897. Their Tramways & Electricity Committee retained Dr. John Hopkinson, a noted electrical engineer, to advise them and also sent delegations on several exploratory visits overseas. As a result it was decided to model the new tramway very closely on that in Hamburg and to use single-deck cars. However, Hopkinson died shortly afterwards and the committee thereafter followed UK practice with double-deck trams.

The first lines were to Dingle and Princes Park Gates and opened in 1898-99. Thereafter expansion was swift and the last horse cars ran in 1902/3, by which time Liverpool had (temporarily) the largest electric tramway in England with over 450 trams. Some of the more important later tramway extensions were to Prescot and St. Helen's (1902, initially privately operated) and Bowring Park (1914/15, on modern reserved track). Over the pre-1914 period competition to the tramways grew. In 1903 the Mersey Railway was electrified, though this was largely a matter affecting the Mersey Ferries as most of the line was either under or on the other side of the river. Rather more significant was the electrification of the Lancashire & Yorkshire Railway's (L&Y) lines from Liverpool Exchange to Southport and Ormskirk between 1903 and 1913 as the company had several suburban stations within the city. The first real motorbus service in the area ran to Woolton (then outside Liverpool) from 1907 and in 1911 it was taken over by the Corporation. A couple more services were added before the First World War, but all were designed to provide connections where there was no tramway. Further expansion occurred after 1919, this time deliberately planned to relieve the tramways which were suffering from a severe lack of maintenance during the war years. It was soon discovered that this was not a wise policy and buses were diverted to run feeder services to tramway termini, though public pressure quickly led again to the provision of some through routes which, once more, proved loss-making. Competition to the trams from within the transport undertaking itself was not, therefore, a real threat at this stage.

Buses operated by outside firms, however, had the potential to become a different matter. Councils then had powers to licence buses within their areas and this was the main tool used to keep competitors at bay. The first major attempt to run services within Liverpool was made by the Merseyside Touring Company in 1929-30, very much hand in glove with Bootle Corporation who used the firm to carry on a long-running feud with their larger neighbour. And even though that fleet name soon disappeared, its routes made a brief reappearance under the McShanes badge in 1932 and a long legal battle was necessary to remove the upstart concern. The major operators were Ribble and Crosville and, in 1929-30, both companies were strengthened by a financial link with the London, Midland & Scottish (LMS) Railway. The Road Traffic Act 1930 removed the power to licence bus routes from councils so greater penetration of Liverpool by the companies was agreed by the three parties. Both the Corporation and the two large companies were given rights to operate buses and to collect fares within certain areas, though this only involved the trams insofar as they were subject to greater competition in the outer districts.

Despite this and, as well as the deleterious effects of inter-war economic problems on Liverpool's economy, the tramway system was developed further, particularly as an adjunct to the city council's policies of slum clearance and the relocation of populations to new housing areas further out of the city. The form the new tram lines took was significantly influenced by John Brodie, the city engineer, whose department was responsible for the tram tracks. He strongly favoured off-road lines, laid within a grassed area and this was one foundation for the truly modern tram system which began to emerge in the early-1930s. Some of the more important extensions were along Mather Avenue and Utting Avenue and to Woolton.

The electric tram fleet displayed both a fascinating variety and also a bewildering series of improvements to existing cars coupled with the replacement of older ones with new ones actually or nominally including parts of the previous ones and therefore taking their numbers. It is not the function of a book like this to chart all these changes. The important ones will be noted as far as possible, but clarity is best served by bearing in mind this simplified progression, much of which was common to all large UK tram systems. However, a unique feature in Liverpool was the early experimental single-deck phase. After that open top double deckers became the norm, as they were on all but the smallest tramways elsewhere. These were all very well, but the British climate, especially on the west coast, does tend to cloud and rain, meaning that the upper deck seats were often effectively unusable. Liverpool was to the fore in developing a viable top deck roof, named the Bellamy cover after the tramways manager of the time. Ground breaking in the early Edwardian era, it was still being built long after other places had developed the improved open balcony type with roofed ends which was finally introduced to Liverpool from 1913 onwards. The next step was to fully enclose the top deck, an improvement put into large-scale production from 1922 onwards. The then general manager, Percy Priestly, was against the final stage of enclosing the drivers' platforms, but this was nevertheless done after 1927. Throughout, virtually the whole fleet had run on four wheels (in tramway parlance, a two-axle truck), but after 1931 most new trams had a pair of bogie trucks on the same principle as railway carriages. The first bogie cars remained fairly traditional in appearance and provide a suitable closing point for this volume. The greater part of Liverpool's trams were built in its own workshops so far as the body went, with electrical equipment and often also trucks being bought in. Within this broad picture there were numerous individual classes of tram, differing names for the same type, as well as one-off or small groups of experimental trams. Where possible this level of detail is brought out in the captions. Tramcar builders and equipment suppliers are listed in an appendix but other concerns, such as railway companies, are shown in full on the first mention and then by abbreviations thereafter.

This volume is intended to show the development of the tramcars and the tram routes until about 1932. A handful of photographs were taken a few years after that, but they are carefully chosen to show what the tramway looked like in the first couple of years of the decade rather than after the system had been transformed by the design and building of many much more modern trams. That story will be told in Volume 2. Much reliance is placed for the early years on commercial postcards which, naturally, tend to have been taken at a limited number of locations, usually within the city centre. So the geographic coverage is not as good as one might wish. The aim remains, however, to illustrate some of the key buildings and streets within what is admitted by all to be a singularly handsome city and, of course, the trams that provided the main means of public transport to Liverpudlians during this period.

The first horse cars were very heavy, based on early American practice, and built by Starbucks of Birkenhead, possibly using American parts. This is probably their second design, being lighter and having far safer stairways. It is on the inward 'loop' track in Church Street. Beyond the horse drawn road vehicles and just visible on the left is St Peter's Church, which gave its name to the thoroughfare. It had been consecrated in 1704 and was said to be the first post-reformation parish church in Lancashire. In 1880 Liverpool became the seat of a bishop and St Peter's became the temporary or pro-cathedral. Once it had been decided to build a new one the valuable city centre site had to be sold to raise funds so St Peter's (generally agreed to be rather ugly) was closed in 1910.

The magnificent St George's Hall (1841-56) forms the background to this view of the Lime Street terminus. The neo-Grecian design was by a young architect, H. L. Elmes, though the rich interiors are largely the work of others appointed after his early death. After only a few decades the ever-present smog of a Victorian city was beginning to settle on the stonework. The sculpture above the portico became unsafe partly for this reason and was removed in 1950. Behind the hall is the Walker Art Gallery on William Brown Street, built about 30 years later. The Bootle horse tram service ran via Scotland Road and Stanley Road to Strand Road.

This horse car is climbing Lord Street and making a turn either into Castle Street or to James Street and Pier Head. Usually double deck trams were hauled by a pair of horses except on steep gradients, where a third 'trace' horse might be added, but Liverpool's hills meant that it was quite usual for three to be required throughout. The tram itself is relatively modern, probably built in the 1890s, with reversible transverse 'garden' seats on the top deck. The ladder propped up against the street lamp was a mobile fire escape, possibly modelled on the provisions of a 1774 Act for fire prevention in London; only in 1891 were new public buildings (except theatres, which were already covered) expected to provide suitable escape routes for higher storeys.

This is the other end of Lord Street at the corner of Whitechapel. The handsome premises along here were erected from the 1820s as some of the first speculative office blocks in Liverpool, not long after this happened in London. Despite appearances, they were never homes. Virtually all were destroyed by bombing in the Second World War. The large building across the end of the street is St George's Church, dating from the 18th century and rebuilt in the early 19th century. Just passing the lamppost in the foreground is a Hansom cab. The two horse cars visible here have knifeboard seats on the top deck, a name taken from a board used for cleaning knives.

George's Pier Head (the contemporary name) probably had the most elaborate horse tram terminus in Britain; in contrast, in most towns services would simply stop in the street. There were five separate tracks and it is possible to see the rare form of centre groove rail used in Liverpool from the mid-1870s; it was thought to give a smoother ride over junctions than the normal side groove type. The glazed cast iron structure to the left was built in 1884 as a shelter for passengers waiting for either ferries – which tied up on the other side – or trams. It was beyond doubt the finest contemporary tram shelter in the UK, more than likely in the world.

This car (above) is at the intersection, marked by a rather splendid gas lamp, of Church Street (in the background), Lord Street, Whitechapel and Paradise Street. The building on the corner behind it included the premises of Foster, Porter & Co., one of many textile warehousemen in the city. Because much of the city centre was too narrow for double lines the horse trams used a long one-way loop to reach Pier Head, inbound cars using Whitechapel/Church Street and Lord Street. This tram is an Eades Reversible type on which the body could be swung on an integral turntable. Most were built by Ashburys in Manchester (John Eades worked for the city's tram company), but a patent action brought by Eades in 1881 indicates that some similar cars were built by Starbucks, and these may have included the Liverpool versions. The example of an Eades truck (below) is kept in 'as discovered' form at the National Tramway Museum, Crich and shows the turntable mechanism.

In 1882 there was a major expansion of services which now reached places like Bootle, North Docks and Princes Park and, on 17th April, the new terminus at George's Pier Head. To reach it trams had to cross a swing bridge over the channel giving access to George's Dock. This photograph was taken after 1892 when, on 4th February, the first section of the Liverpool Overhead Railway was ceremonially commissioned by the Marquis of Salisbury (sometime Prime Minister). This was the only example in the UK of an elevated railway. The tram company built a number of single-ended cars themselves, including this one dating from the 1880s with an extra seat on the front platform and, above it, an elliptical awning. Probably fearing further legal action, they dispensed with the turntable; special reversal facilities were needed at termini.

The outward part of the loop ran along Dale Street. Car 173 was probably built during the 1880s at the company's own workshops. The trams were normally always used on the same routes, so the destination – Walton via Scotland Road – is painted on the dash plate and stair riser. The man in the bowler hat upstairs is sitting sideways as the car still has a knifeboard seat on the top deck, as did most cars built for the system in the 1880s. This already somewhat old-fashioned style was probably retained to save weight.

A traffic jam was not usual on a horse tramway but on 22nd June 1897 outbound cars along Dale Street were held up by the local celebrations for Queen Victoria's Diamond Jubilee. The second car in the top view is probably another of the Eades type, one of the few innovations Liverpool ever deigned to borrow from its rival city! The original knifeboard seat, seen in the earlier view, has been replaced by transverse ones presumably, in this case, not reversible (that wasn't needed). Many top deck passengers have their parasols up to shield them from the sun. The other photograph was quite likely taken on the same day as the horse drawn-vehicles on the right (corporation carts?) are all decorated with bows and ribbons. This tram is just passing the Municipal Buildings on Dale Street, built in Renaissance style in 1862-8 and still today the main point of public access for enquiries about council services. The style has something of a French feel about it.

This is the Seaforth Sands route on 25th May 1894 at Derby Road Bridges, which crossed one of dock railway branches. The bobby from the Liverpool City Police seems to exude authority. This professional force was formed in 1836. The tram is one of a small series built especially for this route in 1892 and, in contrast to most, with transverse seats from the start. Like the entire fleet, it was liberally covered with route information on the dash, stair stringer, above and below the windows and on a route board above the driver's head. Passengers could travel to, for example, North Docks, Mill Street and Vauxhall Road. In company days advertisements were also displayed on heavy cast iron plates but after the Corporation takeover, these were removed.

Horse traction was not economic as the animals cost a great deal to buy, feed, house and provide with veterinary care. Between 1879 and 1890 experiments were made with various other forms of traction in the UK, including compressed air, steam, cable and accumulator. However Liverpool, like nearly all other towns, decided on electrification. The final horse cars, of this pattern, were turned out from the tramway works at Lambeth Road in 1897. Six miles of route lay in Bootle and three quarters of a mile in Litherland, both then being independent urban districts (UDCs). Relations between them and Liverpool were never good and Litherland refused to compromise over the rental the city should pay for its short length of track. As a result one horse car had to shuttle up and down here until 25th August 1903. Car 330 was photographed in Linacre Road at the Bootle end, probably around 1902.

Trial running on the first electric tram route to Dingle took place in October and November 1898. Because the council delegation had decided to emulate the Hamburg tramways they bought some trams from German builders. Hamburg, however, had not one but two company operated lines and Liverpool purchased cars duplicating those used by both. One type, illustrated in these two pictures of drivers under instruction, were known as Ringbahn (for circular service) cars and were pretty typical of continental practice prior to the First World War. They were operated on the *Strasseneisenbahn-Ges.* in Hamburg from 1894. Again following European practice, the city council purchased trailers as well as powered cars. The first view shows motor tram 426 turning from Canning Place into Park Lane. In the rear is the Custom House, built in 1828-39 on the site of the filled-in Old Dock and one of the city's finest buildings. It was burnt out during the blitz of 1941 and demolished after the war 'to create employment'; restoration would have secured far more jobs! The second view includes 424 and a trailer running along Park Lane. The overhead wiring was supported by pillars like that on the left. The elegant cast iron work at the base served no practical purpose and was removed in almost all cases as part of the the Second World War scrap drive. Despite the presence of electricity, the new lamps were still fed by gas.

This interesting postcard shows Hamburg tram 756 on the Ringbahn in 1905. It is just turning across a major crossroad where traffic – not that there is much! – is under the control of the policeman standing beside the tram. In fact, the only other road vehicle is the large cart. A typical Continental feature is the advertisement column at the extreme right. Liverpool bought the earliest type of car (the Hamburg ones were built in their workshops at Falkenried in 1894-97) and though this is a later and slightly larger model, built 1904-06, it closely resembles the Liverpool cars. From 1897 to 1927 Hamburg tram routes usually had a symbol, such as a star in different colours, or else a letter to supplement the route number; the Ringbahn was therefore number 26 and route R.

The first electric depot was at Dingle, from 16th November 1898 the terminus of the initial route A, further extended to Aigburth Vale on 24th April 1899. This view inside the tram shed shows how varied the early fleet was. The second type of German car heads the third row of trams. 406 was also based on a Hamburg prototype, that used by the *Hamburg-Altonaer Centralbahn-Ges.* Its quite unique curvilinear style led to that company being christened the *Chinesenbahn* (Chinese railway). Behind it and on the extreme right are further Ringbahn cars. Both came from the same German manufacturers, Busch and Schuckert. Next to 406 is 442, a long bogie tram built by what became America's biggest streetcar manufacturer, Brill of Philadelphia. At the back are three far more typical British trams, those known in Liverpool as the BTH type.

The Centralbahn ran west to east across Hamburg's Altstadt (old town) from Berliner Tor via Millerntor to Ottensen. The latter was in the then-independent town of Altona. It was a highly lucrative route and the company retained its independence until 1922/23. This card shows two of its distinctive motor trams – running without trailers – at Mönkerbergstrasse/Rathausstrasse near the Berliner Tor terminus in Hamburg proper. The rectangles on the dashes displayed the destination. The car in the foreground illustrates the exceptionally deep clerestory roof, giving a quite different appearance from the Ringbahn trams. The card was probably written by a wounded soldier in 1915 as it is stamped 'field post' and postmarked 'reserve hospital VII'. All this area was destroyed in the British and American fire storm raids in late July 1943.

Route B to Princes Park Gates was the second electric route to be opened, on 15th January 1899. This is the dead-end terminus at St. George's Crescent immediately after that. Until early 1899 the motor tram had to leave its trailer in the street, run back past it, reverse, and then finally re-secure the couplings. For a short while motor and trailer sets were made up of cars with consecutive numbers, like 411 and 412 here. American bogie car 435 is on route B and the two-axle trams are on route A. After 24th April a loop line was opened via Lord Street (on the left) which allowed the coupled trams to run through. The wheeled contraption in the foreground is another mobile fire escape.

It was thought that double deck trams would need to stop whilst passengers climbed the stairs, an unacceptable delay, one reason why the initial purchase was of single deckers. This was not a problem, however, and the small cars were found to be uneconomic to run and were all withdrawn within two years. Some were converted into works vehicles, including 418 and 424, which became cash vans in 1905. At this period conductors paid in their cash at terminals where the vans collected it and, from 1907, took it via a special track right into the Hatton Gardens Head Office. One can be seen on the left in this Pier Head view, probably taken in the 1920s. Behind is the busy river, with cargo boats passing up and down and a passenger ship loading at the landing stage.

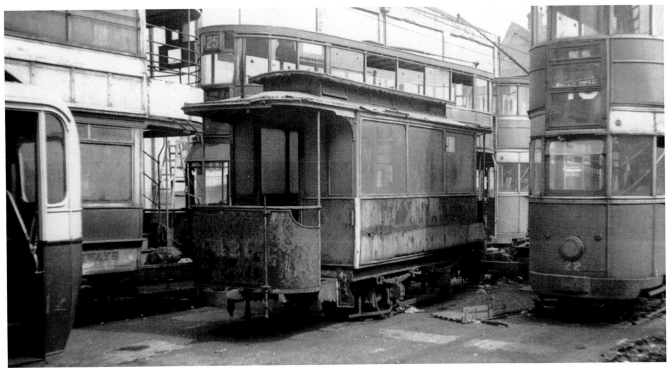

Ringbahn trailer 429 became a stores car at Garston Depot and there it stayed, almost completely unaltered, for half a century. Eventually it was taken to Edge Lane Works to be scrapped. This unique vehicle (in British terms) was the subject of a preservation attempt, but this came to nothing and it was broken up. The small saloon had seated 18 passengers and a few more could stand on the open platforms. The trams surrounding it are mostly of the inter-war fully enclosed type.

Above: Many of the buildings on Lord Street and Church Street are decorated with bunting and flags, probably for Edward VII's Coronation. The car in the rear is 380, in service from April 1901, and typical of the fleet once the experimental period was over. The American tram nearer the camera had a centre entrance and two separate saloons, originally designed to accommodate 1st and 2nd class passengers separately. All, like the German cars, were delivered in 1898. Most went in the 1920s but three lasted until 1933. They were converted with lengthened platforms, stairs and top deck seating, giving a total authorised capacity of 124, far more than any other trams in Liverpool before or since.

Opposite: The other type of tram ordered in the experimental phase had a double deck and open top, a general design used widely on British tramways prior to the First World War. 455 and 458 were part of this small series of twelve ordered in 1898 from British Thomson Houston (BTH) with bodies by the Birkenhead firm of Milnes and American trucks from Peckham. 458 is running on the extended Lord Street to Aigburth Vale line and behind it is Altona trailer 413. Double deckers never had the route letters used by the single deckers. The cars had no roof over the driver's head (that is, they were uncanopied). The passengers stepped straight off the stairs and platform when exiting (a design known as the direct stair). Saloon curtains were fitted, but these were soon discarded as unhygienic. Slung over the top rail in the first photograph are oilskins provided for upper deck passengers (like on the horse cars), but this provision was quickly withdrawn. The second picture shows two of the series immediately after delivery in Dingle Depot and before they had had their trolley poles erected. The Smithdown Road route, the third, was opened on 9th July 1899. The early trams were all numbered from 400 upwards to follow the horse cars (though with an unfilled gap).

This is Lord Street in all its late Victorian elegance, photographed between April and September 1899. BTH/Milnes car 449, which has just left the South Castle Street terminus, positively sparkles in its new paintwork. The driver is under instruction. The man chatting to a friend is seated on a fixed bench but everyone else will be able to use one of the garden seats to face the direction of travel. At the end of the street is St George's Church which was built by 1726 on the site of Liverpool Castle by Thomas Steer, the dock architect, and thought then to be one of the most handsome edifices in the city. It had been closed in 1897 and was demolished a few months after this photograph was taken. Ecclesiastical – or indeed municipal – vandalism is not new.

The north end of today's Pier Head was described earlier as either the Landing Stage or St. Nicholas Place. To the left are warehouses standing beside a dock. Next is Our Lady & St. Nicholas, Liverpool's parish church, originally dating back to the 13th or 14th centuries but much rebuilt. The tower was used as a navigational mark for shipping. The two bridges carried the Liverpool Overhead Railway tracks, this being the world's first electric overhead line, the older New York 'El' being steam-operated at the time; passengers were carried from 6th February 1893. Of the two trams facing the camera the left hand one is a BTH car going to Bootle, a route electrified on 25th November 1900.

The tram terminus was, of course, on dry land, but the landing stage was a floating structure; note the anchor chain in the foreground helping to secure it. 'Stages' was more precise and this is George's Landing Stage with Prince's Stage in the background, though by the end of the 19th century they had been joined together. After further extension in the following decade their total length was not far short of a half a mile. Transatlantic liners docked at the further point whilst Mersey ferries and Isle of Man steamers used the nearer end. What look like tram lines on the floating bridge are kerbs to guide horse-drawn wagons.

BTH car 454 is pictured in 1899, probably at Smithdown Road. Due to lack of experience in the UK industry the Peckham cantilever truck was imported from America. It was remarkably well sprung and must have given quite a bouncy ride. Everyone, including the child on the bottom step, is 'watching the birdie'. The crew includes the driver on the front platform, a conductor with his strap to carry his cash bag, and a third man, an inspector or driving instructor. Safety upstairs is assured by the wire mesh fixed to the railings and, downstairs, domesticity reigns with curtains at the windows. 454 carries its original number but after September all cars (except the withdrawn German ones) were renumbered from No. 1 upwards, the BTH trams becoming 21-32.

Once electrification had proved itself and the decision had been taken to standardise on double deck trams, the aims of the tramways department were threefold – to electrify the remaining horse services, to expand coverage to new parts of the city and to expand the fleet as rapidly as possible. The next line to exchange animal for electrical power was that to Walton, on 5th November 1899. The initial terminus was at South Castle Street but, by the date of this photograph, cars ran through to Pier Head. It is 9th August 1902, the day when Edward VII was crowned, the bunting is up and the ladies are in their finery. The car, one of the BTH/Milnes ones, is outside the Town Hall; Dale Street is to the right and Water Street to the left.

The tramcar fleet was initially expanded by some further limited trial purchases, the first of which was a small series of cars from the Westinghouse Company, then based in America but soon to open a factory in the north west of England. They manufactured only electrical equipment so it was their practice to subcontract the bodies to a UK firm, in this case Brush. The trucks were, however, imported from the Peckham Co. of New York. Later the designer, Edgar Peckham, moved to England to design rather more sophisticated running gear. The Westinghouse cars arrived, as 459-463, in midsummer 1899 and in September were renumbered 43-47. The canopy headlights were brought down to the dash, accounting for the fact that the fleet number was displaced sideways. 44 is shown in Water Street during another major celebration.

British-based companies gradually began to be able to offer trams complete with electrical equipment and the next few cars were provided 'ready to run' by Brush of Loughborough (oddly, a town which never had a tramway of its own). 464-468 naturally had similar bodies to the Westinghouse cars. The first of them is seen on the Aigburth Road extension from Dingle which was largely single track. However these five trams were sent back to the manufacturers within a few months, presumably due to deficiencies in their British-made electrical equipment. They were then sold on to Leeds which used them – though not without problems – until the mid-1920s.

The next trial order was for ten cars of this pattern from Dick, Kerr. Of the three types tested, this was considered the best and a total of 91 were added to the fleet during 1899 and 1900. The first ten were given the old 'horse tram' numbers and 470 is pictured outside Dingle Depot. Although the stairs had the normal curved form the class were always known as the Straight Stair (or, by the staff, 'Little Emma') type to distinguish them from the later design of car which became standard in Liverpool. 470 has its headlamp mounted above the driver's head, from where it was soon moved to the dash. It also has a drawbar for hauling a trailer, a plan which was never put into effect.

This view of Lord Street comes from the turn of the century as both trams are of the same early design. No. 123 on the left is heading in towards either Castle Street or the Landing Stage. The conductor is standing on the rear platform, perhaps assisting the passenger who is just boarding. Photographs in those days were taken at a relatively slow speed which was unable to 'freeze' the early motor car on the right. The nearest shop to it belongs to the Milner Safe Company, a relatively rare example of a Liverpool-based manufacturing concern. Oddly, perhaps, the founder had moved across from a centre of the iron and steel trade, Sheffield, in 1830. At one time the company was believed to be the largest safe maker in the world and, later, had a factory at Speke.

The tram in the foreground was delivered with 'new' number 80 and is running on one of the initial electric routes, near Princes Park. This is a unique 'double boulevard', with Princes Road (1840s) on one side of the central island and Princes Avenue (1870s) on the other. The earliest houses were the yellow brick ones on the right. They were intended for prosperous residents and a variety of churches were built to serve them. The steeple belongs to the (derelict) Welsh Presbyterian church. In 1870 an Orthodox Church was built in the area to serve the city's growing Greek community and there is also a synagogue. The tram lines ran along only one of the two carriageways. Many of the larger houses were later replaced by rows of smaller terraces and the remaining bigger dwellings split up into multi-occupancy.

A pair of 'Little Emmas' pass each each at the top of Church Street. Car 99, on the left, is heading for Dingle and the other is inbound to Pier Head. The exceptionally clear route indicators here look like destination blinds but they are in fact four-sided rotating boxes into which glass slides were placed; they were illuminated at night. On the corner of Whitechapel is the famous Bunney's department store which specialised in oriental goods brought to Liverpool as return cargoes from the Far East. They also had a branch in Llandudno. Opposite here is a building originally known as Seel House, a fairly rare example of commercial architecture designed by E. W. Pugin, much better known for his Roman Catholic churches.

Electrification of the horse tramways to Aintree and Fazakerley was completed ready for service on 11th February 1900 and Straight Stair car 65 is running along Warbreck Moor, Aintree, three and a half years later. Most of these early pictures are taken from postcards which can often only be dated circumstantially from, for example, the dates of posting. It is rare to find a photograph from this period with a precise date like this one. Within three decades this sylvan scene of pleasant villas facing parkland was to be transformed by much more dense development aided by the better transport provision to Liverpool given by the trams.

During 1899 the Corporation built six trams at Lambeth Road, a first attempt at electric rather than horse vehicles. They were numbered 479-484 (the last before renumbering, to 48-53). A distinguishing feature was stairs with a landing halfway down, intended to make descending safer; hence the sinuous curve of the 'banisters' in this view. Another was the two very large saloon windows. The car is making its way off the Seaforth route into a crowded Church Street from Ranelagh Street. The use of a side bracket arm for the overhead was fairly uncommon in Liverpool, but there were some similar ones in Knotty Ash and Bootle. 48 ex-479, which had first run on 7th July 1899, survived with two others until 1950 in a much-rebuilt form as a Gateshead tram.

An experiment with a single-ended car was made in 1901 with locally-built car 5 which was unique. It was very long and high, had four instead of the usual three windows and was fitted with an American Curtis truck. It was not a success and was soon re-equipped for double-ended operation. In 1902 one of the German cars was fitted with lights to run as an illuminated car for Edward VII's Coronation, such cars becoming a popular feature before 1914. No. 5 may have been running for the same event or possibly in connection with the visit of some Indian troops on 28th July. The Tramways Band are entertaining the crowds from the top deck.

In 1899-1900 the works turned out seven other cars to designs by the general manager. One closely resembled this one and 200 were ordered from ER&TC, Preston. All were delivered within one year, 1900. Eventually there were 305 of this Preston class. The majority were built in the eponymous town but the bodies of many more were constructed at Lambeth Road. Conversion of the horse tramway to Cabbage Hall (at the far end of Breck Road) took place on 9th January 1900. The famous range of buildings on William Brown Street originally included the Technical School, which later became part of the museum and library.

One of that first batch of Preston cars is coming down Castle Street to the crossing with Lord Street. The photograph is rather indistinct but is historically interesting, showing the city all done up with flags and streamers. This is probably either 26th June or 9th August 1902, the planned or actual dates of King Edward VII's coronation. Illness forced a postponement, but local celebrations were so advanced that they still went ahead. Edwardian dress codes were far removed from today's jeans culture. All the men are wearing suits and hats, the lady and her daughter are attired in elegant dresses and millinery and the young lad in the centre foreground sports knickerbockers.

The trams passing the hotel owned by the London & North Western Railway (LNWR) on Lime Street are only *just* visible. To the right is one of the rather scruffy buildings which obscured the soaring station arch until very recently. However, the card is included because of the comment on it, "bags carried free of charge – please note that these cars are not run on the Cable system." The writer was probably a Scot from Edinburgh, where their trams were cable-hauled, like San Francisco's. The correspondent found Liverpool "a miserable place" (it was "raining hard") and would "much rather have (had) the Caledonian". This could have been a reference to the *Caledonia*, a ship of the Anchor Line which served New York from Glasgow; or maybe the writer regretted having left the warm fug of the Caledonian Vaults in Lime Street!

LORD STREET LIVERPOOL

Preston car 208 demonstrates its two major innovations, the continuation of the roof over the platforms, which gave the crew some cover and allowed for six extra seats on top – and the use of reversed stairs, known locally as Bellamy stairs, after the manager who had introduced them (though they were used elsewhere and were not his invention). The idea was that descending passengers would not be catapulted into the road if the car had to stop suddenly! When used in other towns these trams were known as the Liverpool type. This is the top of Lord Street at the junction with Castle Street and South Castle Street. The photographer has probably drawn in the overhead wiring, a common ploy when the print did not show it clearly.

This gives an excellent close-up of Preston car 325. Working down from the top, the car has a long trolley pole; once a roof was fitted, it could be shorter. Hexagonal route indicators have been fitted and the lettering visible means 'via Myrtle Street'. The shadows thrown by the pedestrians indicate a sunny day, so the upstairs passenger is using a parasol rather than an umbrella. The seating is surrounded by iron railings and wire mesh for safety reasons. The car has the standard three-window saloon in which there were eleven seats along each side. The products advertised can still be bought now, but the Empire Theatre, on Lime Street, would not be today's but the older building opened as the New Prince of Wales Theatre and Opera House in 1866.

260, further down Lord Street, is running to North Docks, out towards Seaforth. The man sitting in relaxed pose on top is using one of the extra seats permitted by the canopy extension; there were 34 upstairs as against 28 on the Straight Stair cars. Unlimited standees were allowed on top at first, most surprisingly, and six and later nine were still permitted under later regulations. When more modern trams appeared in the 1930s standing passengers were only permitted on the lower deck. Milkmaid 'full cream' Milk was what we would call condensed milk and it is still sold by Nestlé in India, where the brand has been available since 1912. On the right-hand side of the street is Dresden House, occupied by Stonier & Co. Their name appears on china recovered from the wreck of the *Titanic*, but they were not manufacturers, only retailers and brokers.

Lord Street, Liverpool

This is again near the top of Lord Street, looking towards Church Street. The tram tracks here led into and out of Castle Street, on the left, and South Castle Street on the right. There was also a pair of tracks straight across between the two and a loop at the end of South Castle Street, allowing cars to turn there without going through to the Pier Head. Two open top Preston cars are on Lord Street.

Car 256 ran from October 1900 and then re-entered service in February 1905 with a roof, so this postcard view was taken between those dates. Dale Street in this era was a handsome thoroughfare bounded here on the right by the Municipal Offices and the Conservative Club. The former was built in a suitably grandiose style for the burgeoning city. The Conservative Club was added in 1882-3. Nowadays a thriving Tory Association seems unlikely, but there was a large Conservative electorate for many years after that. As late as 1955 every single councillor was Conservative and the city had eight Tory MPs, but by 2006 the party had not one elected representative from or in the city. Long-term demographic changes have contributed to this but so did the social earthquake of the 1980s.

The three-legged sign on the right-hand building indicates the Legs of Man pub which stood on the corner of Lime Street and London Road; it has only fairly recently been demolished to make way for an extension to the (new) Empire Theatre, a little further down Lime Street. London Road was then a thriving shopping area. It is ten to three on an Edwardian summer's afternoon. Both ladies and gentlemen are wearing straw boaters, some of the former, perhaps, heading across the road to buy a parasol from Crawford's, on the opposite corner, manufacturers of umbrellas, parasols and sticks. Preston tram 173 does not yet have any form of destination indicator except for the side boards; additional paper labels might have been pasted on the dashes or windows.

On reaching a terminus the former German power cars either had to 'run round' their trailers, as they did at South Castle Street, go round a turning loop as they were later able to do via Lord Street or, alternatively, at Dingle Terminus they were able to push their trailers back into a 'wye' to reverse the tram set as a whole. A Preston car later found the turning facility useful for reversing with a works trailer, one of a number built specially to distribute rock salt along the tracks to melt snow. The very earliest double deckers had been equipped with drawbars, as it had still been the intention to haul passenger trailers (never actually done), but Preston cars did not have them so the two vehicles (seen here in 1902) are connected by a chain.

Open top Preston trams stand on the terminal loop at St. Nicholas Place at the turn of the century. There is a crossover track between two of the lines which would allow a rear car to overtake if necessary. A Liverpool Overhead Railway train can be faintly discerned on the viaduct. The tram track behind the Overhead Railway was required to reach the main city streets. The car under the bowstring bridge is a 'Little Emma'. Beside the loop is a rank filled with Hansom cabs. A line of gas lamps alongside the tram terminus show how street lighting lagged behind transport. In fact, gas lamps were still fairly common on side streets in poorer areas right up until the 1950s. The fine tower and lantern of St. Nicholas, added around 1811-15, alone survived the blitz.

An enlargement of the above view shows car 341, the last of the original tranche of 200 ordered from Dick, Kerr which entered service in early 1901. By then the cars were equipped with a new-style destination indicator consisting of a hexagonal device fitted with six glass slides, the whole being capable of rotation as required. It was lit at night. Reading the display from photographs is not easy because usually only one destination shows, whereas passengers were intended to see two, one showing the final terminus and the other a point passed en route. In this case the car will be running via Myrtle Street, which was never a terminus, to either Croxteth Road or Smithdown Road, both of which were new extensions made beyond the old horse tramway and opened on 3rd May 1900.

All these early cars suffered from the very exposed position for top deck passengers. C. R. Bellamy, the general manager, experimented with various contraptions and eventually settled on this version which consisted of a light framework erected within the upper deck rails, glazed ends, a stout plank to hold the trolley pole and canvas screens for both roof and windows. Bellamy believed in the virtues of fresh air and expected passengers to open the blinds when it was not raining. This is the very first example, 472, photographed in Harlech Street outside Walton Depot in late summer 1902. Other operators sent parties to see the covered trams and Hull, for example, bought sixteen of the developed design (known there as a Magrini cover, probably the name they were patented under), though they also bought a rival design.

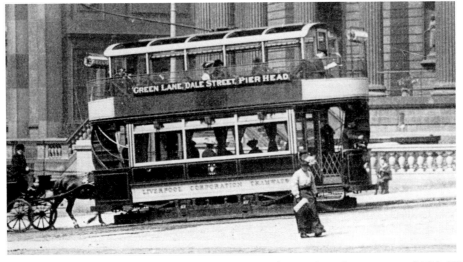

Even ten years later the Hong Kong Tramways were introducing a simpler version of a canvas roof. This ERTC tram, climbing past the Picton Library on William Brown Street, illustrates how such cars could provide a breezy and pleasant ride on a summer's day. The structure seems to end halfway down, which is because it is built within the upper deck railings. The roof was supported on curved steel angle bars fitted to each edge of the upper deck. Though based on the Preston type, from here on this design will be referred to as the Bellamy car. The Green Lane route opened on 21st October 1900, part of the very rapid expansion of the tramway to all parts of the city.

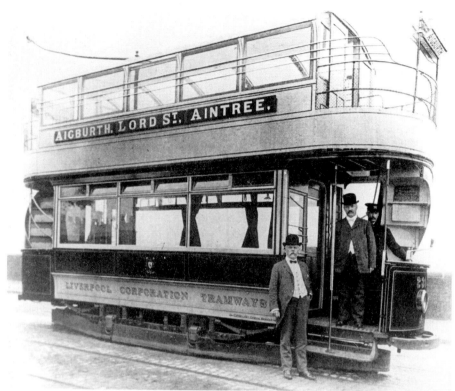

Despite its makeshift nature the canvas cover was a success but it did have faults. It was not fully weatherproof and passengers must have had difficulty seeing where they were. So in 1903 a variant with glazed sides and curved wooden slides in the roof was introduced and this immediately superseded the canvas contraptions. Car 230, which had just received its new cover, was photographed for an article in the 'house magazine' of the municipal tramway industry, the *Tramway & Railway World*. The occasion was the 1904 Municipal Tramways Conference, which was held in Liverpool. Besides the driver, the two men pictured are the general manager, Bellamy (at street level) and C. W. Mallins, the traffic superintendent who, after Bellamy's sudden death, was promoted to fill the vacancy.

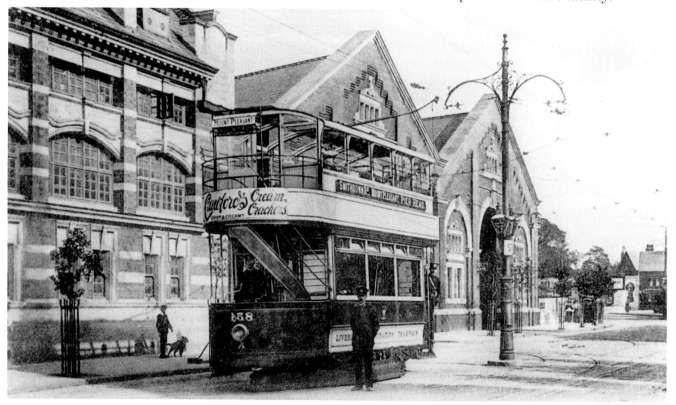

Bellamy 158 displays the top cover in 'open' position. It can be seen that the 'trolley plank' along the centre of the roof was quite broad. Removing the trolley standard from the seating area helped to make it possible to increase the top deck capacity by five passengers which, coupled with the all-weather protection, meant that these cars earned more per mile than open ones did. 158 is standing at Smithdown Road Depot during the time that this formed a terminus. Mount Pleasant was a street fairly near the city centre used by this service on its way to/from the terminus. The first shed at Smithdown Road was opened in 1899 and the second in 1901-2.

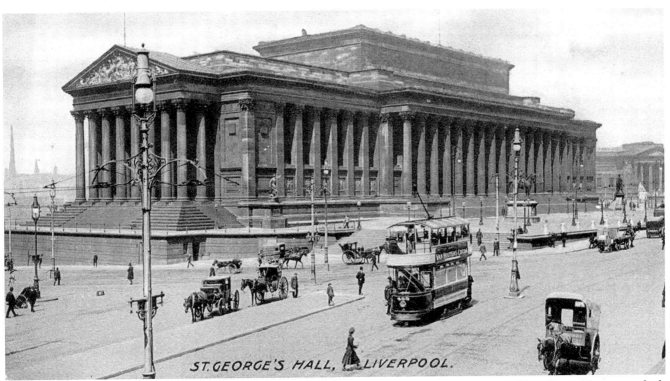

ST. GEORGE'S HALL, LIVERPOOL.

This postcard view of St. George's Hall shows a Bellamy car just pulling away from a stop on Lime Street. Its upper deck windows and roof panels are retracted. Maybe the Edwardian summer was a reality rather than an imagined golden era? The Grade 1 listed building was the result of a competition for a hall suitable for the music festivals held in the city in the early 19th century. Niklaus Pevsner, the architectural historian, described it as one of the finest neo-Grecian buildings in the world. Because of the former law courts within it, there are cells in the basement! Most of the building was opened in 1854. The organ was built by 'Father' Willis, one of the most famous Victorian makers in the world; as Henry Willis & Sons this Liverpool firm is still active today.

The success of the Bellamy cover meant that the period when all Liverpool double deckers had open tops was very short, lasting only from 1899 to 1902. This card of Dale Street was posted in August 1908 and the writer hoped that the recipients, who lived in nearby Southport, were "in the Pink of Condition"! However the photograph itself must have been taken before February 1904 when Preston car 412, in the middle left, had a cover added (all were dealt with by June 1905). The leading tram is 26, one of the BTH cars which were the first double deckers in the fleet. They were all withdrawn by 1920 and later scrapped without ever having even the most rudimentary cover for top deck passengers.

Another comparison between new and old shows Bellamy 159 and Straight Staircase 68 in Lord Street. The white on black indicator is exceptionally easy to read, but this seems to have been an experimental type introduced around the turn of the century, possibly only on these cars. The norm became black on white as displayed by 159. Wood Abrahams opticians leave no doubt as to their business – even to the illiterate! The original partnership between Abraham Abrahams, part of the city's 5,000 strong Jewish community, and George Wood seems to have specialised more in the manufacture of scientific instruments such as microscopes.

Pier Head, Liverpool.

A significant event of this early period was the expansion of the St. Nicholas Place loop in 1901-2 into the Pier Head terminus, made possible by the infilling of George's Dock. Thereafter there were two turning circles, two tracks the full length of the terminus and a third from the north loop and via the second before joining the pair of through lines. Trams are running south to north along the last-named nearest the ferry terminal building and north to south along the 'through' tracks. Small sailing vessels were still seen on the Mersey but Edith's comment on her card, written in 1905, better reflects the contemporary scene: "We have been here today and saw a boat preparing to start for America."

Pier Head has just become the Walton terminus as Castle Street has been pasted over on the side of 481 (still with an 'old' number), one of the small Lambeth Road batch from 1899. It had saloon curtains when new. The other electric car is the later Preston design, the first 26 of which had been delivered by July 1900. The last horse tram route (except for Litherland) was electrified on 7th May 1902 but some horse trams continued to run with electric cars until the end of that year. Number 307 had garden seats and was built at Lambeth Road, being the final type of Liverpool horse tram.

Over 1902-3 the Liverpool Corporation Tramways (LCT) built a dozen cars of the Preston pattern in their own workshops, the first not from ERTC. Six came as new with top covers, 447 being the last. Some Preston-built cars were also covered at delivery. It is easy to see how the design effectively 'dropped in' a roof onto to what was, in origin, an open-topped tramcar. In the right background is the overhead railway Pier Head Station.

This is a close-up of the station. All the others were above ground too, except for Dingle, which was underground. Here and at Seaforth – both busy stops – passengers had to buy their tickets before ascending the stairways. Awnings were usually absent on platforms, but because Pier Head was so busy it was fully enclosed to give protection against cold winter winds coming off the river. In the foreground is one of the elegant tram standards in the centre of the tracks leading to Water Street. Behind are the towers of the parish church and Tower Buildings.

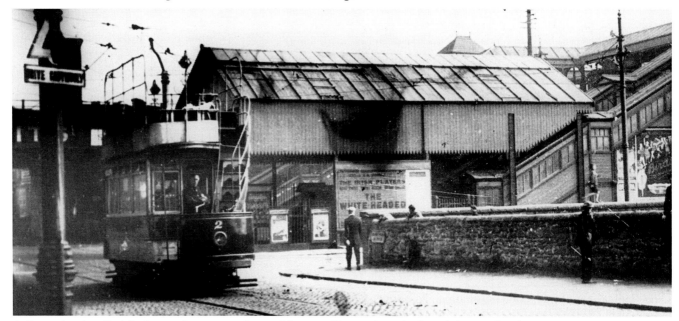

A digression is called for here. There was a demand for travel beyond Seaforth and the two local UDCs, Waterloo and Great Crosby, decided to promote a tram route. They did not want to run it and the Liverpool Overhead Railway thought it would make a logical extension of their railway. The councils provided the track and cars, which the company leased. The single line opened about halfway on 19th June 1900 and throughout by October. Cars 1-8 were similar to the 'Little Emmas'. No. 2 is standing at Seaforth terminus in front of the Overhead station. Trams actually terminated in the large shed, so rail passengers could walk down the stairs and straight on to a waiting tram, one of the first examples in the country of a transport interchange.

Cars 9 and 10 were single deck open-sided vehicles of the type known as crossbench. They were far more suitable to the seaside than to Merseyside! They would have seen only limited use. This is probably near St. John's Road, Waterloo, even though the photographer thought it was a little further on, in Crosby. The fancy ironwork found on Liverpool's centre poles is replicated here on the side poles. Although the track was single, there was a wire for each direction of travel. The houses here were expensive villas, so this was an area where the middle classes who worked in Liverpool's thriving commercial sector lived.

This is a fairly early view of car 7 on Crosby Road, Waterloo. Nos. 1-8 were all delivered with headlamps mounted on the ends of the top deck, a common arrangement with trams at this period and one shared with the Liverpool's BTH, Westinghouse and (the very first) Straight Staircase cars. The telegraph pole on the far side of the road is an interesting feature. In the early days of the telephone each house connected required separate wiring to the exchange. The number of crossbars and insulators indicates how many houses had telephones in the area, an immediate measure of prosperity. Beyond here the route was rather less built-up and there were plenty of trees, like those in the cemetery in the background.

The halfway point was known as Five Lamps, Waterloo, after the elegant lighting standard next to the tracks. Single lines like this – and even Liverpool had a few such sections – needed pointwork and short double track loops every now and again to allow cars to pass. Nos. 13 and 14 were ordered in 1900 and, like the last two from the 1899 batch, had reversed stairs and canopy covers like the Liverpool Prestons. The entire fleet came from Dick, Kerr of Preston. The wiring on the Liverpool Overhead Railway tramway was suspended at one side of the road, meaning the trolley sometimes had to extend a long way across the carriageway. This was why very high railings were provided so passengers were not inadvertently struck by either the trolley or the rope required to pull it round at termini. The second photograph shows the next passing loop at South Road with original car 1 standing next to 14. The wooden waiting room was erected a little while after the opening. The building in the background is a public house.

A delightful Edwardian scene of a group of girls waiting for the tram. The poster advertises cheap first class shopping tickets available for a through journey by tram (which had no first class accommodation) and the Overhead Railway. At the bottom it mentions an electric lift, which was actually a very early escalator which had been installed at Seaforth Sands Station.

The Overhead Railway-operated tramway terminated here, at Great Crosby, where car 4 is standing – literally – at the end of the line. On the left is a type of shop then found in every district but fairly rare now, a local baker's; the only thing that hasn't changed is the availability of Hovis bread. The youngsters with bicycles and baskets may have been delivery boys for Mr. Alcock. The building on the right is a public house. Thorougood's was a local firm based at the Lion Brewery, Waterloo, where, amongst other beers, they made Waterloo Ales.

Even though it is chronologically out of order the story might as well be concluded here. Immediately after the First World War top covers were fitted to a majority of the cars, including 14, seen here at Waterloo. Despite having incurred this expenditure, the Overhead Railway was not allowed to renew its lease and the councils hoped instead to negotiate a connection with the Liverpool system at Seaforth. However, no agreement was reached and the trams stopped running at the end of 1925.

The Garston & District Tramways Co. also intended to run trams outside the boundary, linking with Liverpool tracks at Aigburth, but before construction was completed Garston was absorbed by the city and the LCT finished off the line, which opened on 28th August 1902. This view is on Aigburth Road a year or so earlier as the car is only running from Lord Street to Aigburth Vale. Note the very short side-arm poles used on this stretch. 58 is one of the Straight Stair class and is in 'as delivered' form without end destination boxes. The crews are also wearing the original type of uniform with 'pill box' caps. Golden Butterfly Cigarettes were made by Hignetts, a Liverpool firm, which in 1901 became one of the founding constituents of Imperial Tobacco, formed to resist American competition.

Experience showed that opening roofs were not called for all that often in the British climate and damp conditions caused the panels to become difficult to move when they *were* needed. So from car 501 of 1908 onwards new ones were built with solid roofs and, over several years, all earlier trams were retrofitted. Number 543, pictured here inside a depot, was one of three cars dating from 1910 built with a slightly wider body than normal, so allowing two rows of transverse seats in the lower saloon instead of the more usual benches. Up to that time, too, the workshops had continued to build trams *as though* they would be open toppers, adding the roof almost as an afterthought. The three were the first to be designed and built as single units.

542 was another of the fairly small batch of 27 Bellamy-roof cars built at Lambeth Road in 1910. Although pictured about a quarter of a century later it still appears more or less as built; the exception is the roller blind indicators which were fitted after 1920. The date has to be after 15th February 1934 as that was when 10B was first used for the existing route from Pier Head to Dinas Lane; before that it had been 10A. It was a short working along the exceptionally long route 10 to Prescot. The car is running past St. John's Gardens, on the right, and towards the Technical School on William Brown Street.

Not only did the LCT build well over 100 new trams prior to 1914 plus numerous Bellamy covers, they also had to maintain the entire fleet. This is probably the paint shop at Lambeth Road Works. The two cars in the background have been given a grey primer prior to repainting and some of the men are holding lettered route boards, another painters' task. The seats were varnished before being refitted in the saloons. Until it was modernised in 1913-14 Lambeth Road was not the most up-to-date facility and access to the upper decks was by means of the rather flimsy stepladders and trestles shown in the photograph. In 1920-21 an old horse tram depot at Wavertree was reconstructed to provide a separate paint shop as Lambeth Road was overcrowded.

Accidents could happen, even with new cars. On 22nd January 1906 car 447 ran away down Leece Street and overturned on the curve leading into Renshaw Street. Cars running via Myrtle Street came down Leece Street to Renshaw Street on their way towards Lime Street. Contributory factors may have been the top cover, which might have made the car more unstable, and the lack of track (rather than wheel) brakes, which Liverpool was slow to adopt. However, despite the light Bellamy cover being reduced to matchwood, there were no fatalities.

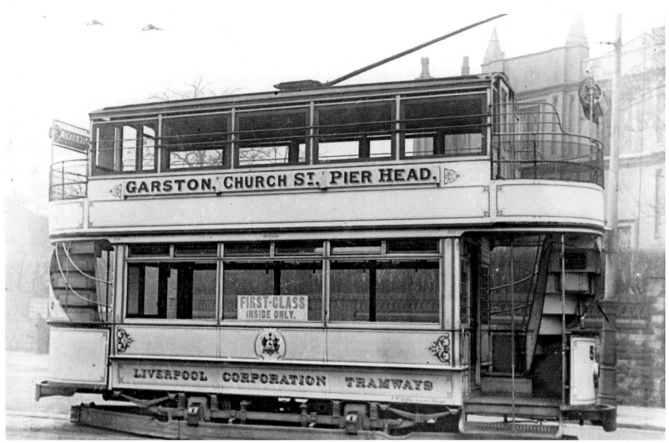

At around the same time it was becoming evident that some middle class people preferred to avoid the trams because they had to share accommodation with working men. So in 1908 an experiment was made with First Class trams on the Garston route. Newly built cars 506-513 were painted in a striking livery of two shades of cream, gold lettering and gold, red and blue lining. A pity there was no colour photography then! The lower saloons were fitted with seats upholstered in blue plush, cut glass light shades and carpets. After some experience it was decided to charge special fares only below as the top deck was unimproved. One of these cars is seen outside Dingle Depot, perhaps in 1909.

The Garston experiment was a success and eventually there were nine First Class services using 67 trams. Car 537 was allocated in June 1910 to the Croxteth Road route. It is seen running to city along Church Street. To the right is the much-blackened St. Peter's Church. Opposite was the first Woolworth's in the UK. To ensure it was not missed the shop title was emblazoned in gilt on red at the usual facia level and at the very top of the building as well. The other sign informed customers that 'Nothing in these stores over 6d', 2.5p in today's money.

Twelve Bellamy-style trams made their appearance in 1912, three of them, 559-561, being given the cream First Class livery. 560 is pictured in this rather atmospheric autumn scene running along Princes Road on the street tracks which occupied a carriageway on one side of the tree-lined central reservation and is on its way back to Pier Head from Croxteth Road. The Bellamy cover for a while put Liverpool at the forefront of tramcar design. Sheffield, for example, did not have any top covered trams until 1905.

This picture was taken near the far end of Church Street. The tram tracks formed a 'Y' because both the succeeding thoroughfares were only wide enough for a single line. Preston 322 has come in along Ranelagh Street; the Bellamy will go out via Elliot and Parker Streets. The large building on the right, by then partially occupied by the Compton Hotel, marks an important milestone in the development of town centres as it was one of the very first purpose-built department stores anywhere in the world. The upper floors included workshops and rooms for live-in staff. It was built for J. R. Jeffrey and opened in 1867. Immediately to the left is the city centre branch of Beatty Bros, Tailors. This firm had stores throughout the North West, one in Market Street, Manchester, for example.

Above: Another First Class route opened on 23 January 1911 to West Derby. This former village had been swallowed up into the city but retained a good deal of its character and included the houses of some of the city's wealthy. The photo shows car 453 on the ordinary service, probably in the first decade of the century. The tracks here included double lines and a crossover, though on the journey to the city there were a few short sections of single line. Beside the tram is the village cross, a faux medieval monument erected in the 1860s with, it is believed, a representation of King John, a significant monarch in the history of both this village and the city itself.

Below: This further view of Princes Road, this time with a Bellamy-roofed car, is some years later than the earlier postcard as the trees have matured. The junction in the foreground led to Catharine Street, the original route to the city centre, or to Upper Parliament Street. In the early days of tramways the overhead wiring was often strung on centre poles like these and Liverpool used them on over sixteen miles of street. The elegant ironwork was typical of Edwardian construction and was topped off by a metal 'plug' to stop water getting inside the steel pole, this one being a typical design of the period known as a ball and finial.

Above: This tram is picking its way over the junctions in William Brown Street. Few routes ever used these as a permanent terminus (in 1913 only Nos. 23 and 24 did so), but it was a useful turn-back point for short workings. The Bellamy car is on the route between Pier Head and Old Swan via Dale Street and Kensington, later route 9. C J van Houten, a Dutchman, invented the process of manufacturing cocoa in 1828. The firm still exists but seems to have withdrawn from the UK market. The tram is passing the the Technical School at the bottom of William Brown Street. The writer reported "splendid weather here", in contrast to the earlier correspondent!

Below: William Brown Street led into London Road, then an extension of the city centre. F. J. Batchelor sold ladies costumes and mantles (dresses), advertised above the first floor windows. The square is called Monument Place, referring to the equestrian statue of George III. The king was unpopular in Liverpool following the loss of America and money came in slowly, so the statue was not unveiled until two years after his death. Rather improbably, the sculptor based it on a statue of the Emperor Marcus Aurelius in Rome, a philosopher and a successful general, neither of which applied to the stolid Hanoverian king. Trams ran along here to such destinations as Old Swan, Everton and West Derby.

There had been a horse tram line along Upper Parliament Street as far as the junction with Smithdown Road but it had never been used by the horse company, even though they had to pay rental to the Corporation for it. The latter controlled the track, but the company did not have to provide uneconomic services. Within a year or so of electrification, however, there were two routes along Smithdown Road itself. One reason for using centrally supported overhead was that frontagers objected to having poles on the pavement or wires attached to their buildings (which were anyway often not strong enough). However it became increasingly evident that they were a hindrance to traffic and those down Smithdown Road were replaced as early as 1906, before the motor age had really got established.

Smithdown Road Depot seems to have attracted postcard photographers, perhaps because it was only the second electric shed to be built and the whole formed an undeniably handsome streetscape. The children are wearing summer clothes and the car's top deck roof and windows are in the open position. At the same location was a refuse destructor which supplied a small part of the power to the city's tramways for many years; renewable energy c.1900! The sheds were later gradually superseded by the new Prince Alfred Road Depot over the period 1928-36, the earlier buildings being turned over to buses.

In 1949 Prince Alfred Road was closed to trams to become a bus garage. Eventually the site was sold and now hosts a small suburban shopping centre. A small part of the building, fronting Smithdown Road, still survives however. Its architectural style is typically 'municipal tramway'. Note the use of skylights to provide daylight within the building, a typical feature of many tram depots.

A later photographer has reproduced the postcard view very closely. It is a summer's day and two window posters encourage people to 'Take the car to Cricket Matches at Aigburth' for a County Match between Lancashire & Leicestershire. Aigburth is home to Liverpool Cricket Club, the oldest amateur sports association in the city. Lancashire used to play there before moving to Old Trafford. The trams provided mass transport to most of the major sporting venues in the city – Liverpool FC, Everton, Aintree Racecourse and the cricket ground.

In much the same quadrant of the city, trams reached Croxteth Road on a short extension from the pioneer electric terminus at Princes Park. 479 is pictured on that route in an area of substantial middle class villas. This type of tram was sometimes known as the covered Preston, alluding to the original design by Dick, Kerr, but in fact the final series actually from the ERTC factory was 453-477, delivered in 1902-3. In the same years the LCT took up the baton with 478-483 and they built all the remainder.

This is Prescot Road at Old Swan. For a short time this was a terminus, but services were extended to Knotty Ash on 25th June 1902 to connect with the (company built and operated) Lancashire Light Railway to Prescot and St. Helens. Between 1900 and 1904 there was also a temporary tram depot on the left hand side of the street. The public house is the Old Swan, dating from 1775 and one of the oldest buildings in the area. It stands on the apex between St. Oswald Street and Broad Green Road. The former later acquired a tramway link through to Edge Lane. The building to the left on the corner of Derbyshire Lane was (and is) a bank.

This view of Fazakerley terminus indicates how far out the trams reached (and the line was extended still further on 23rd July 1923). Postcard photographers, naturally, tended to concentrate their efforts on the city centre with its busy streets and fine buildings, but the trams also ran to quite rural areas like this (described as "a quaint little place" on the card). At the time, Fazakerley was not a part of Liverpool proper, but the trams could expect to attract middle class commuters and ladies going shopping from here as well as working people when the route passed through Walton on the way into the city.

Strand Road, Bootle, was in the same direction though not quite as far outside Liverpool proper. The street runs between Stanley Road and Derby Road/Rimrose Road. It was used by only one regular service, route 23 between Old Haymarket and Seaforth. At this period it was a busy shopping street and quite narrow, so some tracks were only single, as in this view, interspersed by passing loops. The bridge in the background carried the L&Y tracks between Liverpool Exchange and Southport. There was (and is) a station just to the left, known then as Marsh Lane & Strand Road.

As well as providing suburban links, the Tramways Department also needed to reach all the key traffic objectives within the city centre. Railway stations were of major importance in this largely pre-motorised age. The three major termini were Central, Exchange and Lime Street. Central was opened by the Cheshire Lines Committee (the 'umbrella' for three railway companies) quite late, in 1874, and had a cramped site on Ranelagh Street, now a car park. In 1892 the Mersey Railway reached an underground station at the same point. A single storey parcels office fronted on to the street with the main station behind it. The next building along the street was the earliest store belonging to Lewis's (a local firm, not John Lewis). At this time trams passed only inbound along a single track with outbound cars using Parker Street.

Exchange Station was originally opened as Tithebarn Street in 1850 and then rebuilt and renamed in 1888 when it became the terminus for the L&Y. Their Southport branch was electrified using a third rail from 22nd March 1904, the first main line electrification in the UK. The station fronted straight on to the pavement of this narrow street, only leaving room for a single tram track, part of which was never doubled. A Straight Stair car passes prior to 1903, when the card was posted; the writer said she was "enjoying myself very much" in Liverpool. This was one of the seven ancient streets of the medieval borough. Exchange closed in April 1977. When redeveloped the facade was retained to front Mercury Court, an office development built in the mid-1980s.

Above: Lime Street was, from 1836, the terminus of the pioneer Liverpool & Manchester Railway, reached by the famous Edge Hill tunnel which was originally rope worked. The station belonged to the LNWR and next to it was their North Western Hotel, built in the style of a French chateau; its portico can be seen on the left here. Today it is a university hall of residence. The First Class car is standing on the lines used as a terminus. The visible face of the indicator shows Bootle; either this was a short working or the other face showed Litherland, which was the final destination of route 28. 504 was one of the 1908 batch of cars built with the fixed version of the top cover. The motor taxicab was a sign of things to come.

Below: Other key traffic generators for the trams were the major city roads, this one being Dale Street, more of a commercial artery than a shopping street. In 1908 the Mutual Life Insurance Co. of New York had offices on this street corner and, at ground level, there was a branch of the then well-known Liverpool tobacconists, Durandu's. All the cars in view have Bellamy roofs. Like the majority of the Prestons, 220 had its added after it had been in service for a while. This view shows clearly the (closed) opening panels in the roof and also how the assembly has been 'dropped' onto the top deck between the railings. It is noticeable how, apart from the trams, city traffic still depends almost totally on the horse.

This is the junction between Lord Street, Church Street, Whitechapel and Paradise Street, again in 1908, and giving a good view of Bunney's distinctive corner site. Double electric tracks have replaced the single horse line along Whitechapel. Once again, the busy streets are filled with horse-hauled carts. Their iron-bound wheels made them extremely noisy. The young lady demonstrates how the bicycle offered both an alternative to the tram and also a new freedom. As usual, there is a traffic policeman at this crossroads. The decorative cast iron pole base adds a touch of elegance to an otherwise utilitarian object. Certainly an improvement on concrete lamp standards!

The same place, perhaps one or two years earlier, and looking along Church Street. Once again, a policeman is on duty, giving directions to a gentleman. Behind him, a street sweeper is at work, a necessary job in the days of horse transport and particularly when ladies' skirts were so long. Police time was increasingly taken up with point duty in busy city centres, but it was not until the mid-1920s that the American invention of automatic traffic lights was introduced to the UK. The china in Bunney's first floor window display includes that Victorian and Edwardian staple of the bedroom – water bowls and jugs. At the time of writing this corner was a building site, the generally decried replacement for Bunneys having been demolished.

Lord Street from Castle Street; the points for the junction can just be seen behind car 306. Despite its importance, the street is quite short from end to end. It was first developed in the 17th century as Lord Molyneux Street (he then being the owner of the castle) but, by the early 19th century, was proving far too narrow. It was widened fourfold by an 1826 Act, a fortuitous improvement of great assistance to the trams 75 years later because it allowed double tracks to be laid down to the Pier Head. James Buchanan set up his whisky business in 1884 and within a few years obtained a royal warrant for Red Seal (today a Diageo brand) to supply both Queen Victoria and her eldest son; quite how much the Queen herself drank is not recorded!

Church Street, and a First Class tram follows two ordinary (for obvious reasons, never described as second class) ones. 510 was one of the initial trial superior cars built in 1908 and must have been photographed then or in 1909. That Liverpool had 'class' can be judged not only by 510 but also by some of the shops in these upmarket streets. To the right are the premises of Henry Miles & Co., Milliners, selling women's hats, gloves etc. Around this time, however, F. W. Woolworth, the founder of the eponymous American store chain, arrived in England seeking premises for his first British store. He was impressed with Liverpool and this shop was vacant. Woolworths opened for a preview on 5th November 1909 and for business the following day.

CHURCH STREET, LIVERPOOL.

Above: This is the same location taken from the opposite direction. Val Smith, the shop next door, was also a milliners. Both buildings are still extant though the shop fronts – of, respectively, a jewellers and a shoe shop – do not look quite as smart. St Peter's Church (opposite) was demolished in 1922. Woolworths then moved across the road and constructed a large purpose-built store. They were nearly prevented from doing so by Harrods, who had also commissioned an architect to prepare plans for the site. Perhaps they concluded that Liverpool's prosperity was already on the wane. Russell's Ltd, at Cathedral Works, were a watch and clock makers. Car 464, on the right, was part of the initial series fitted from new with glazed and opening covers. 245 received its cover after first running as an open-topper.

Below: The trams here performed a stately dance as they negotiated the sinuous curves leading into Church Street from Ranelagh Street, still single track at the time. 159 was one of the first Preston cars to be delivered in 1900 but was towards the end of the queue to receive a top cover. The sides and roof are open on what must have been a fairly warm day, though there is not much sign of summer clothes being worn. The department store and hotel in the right background now forms the premises of the main city branch of Marks and Spencer's, *sans* the chateau-style pitched roofs.

Above: Lord Street, looking towards Church Street. The approaching car is Bellamy 244 which came into service in October 1900 and was covered in November 1904. It was withdrawn from traffic in July 1937. The car behind is a Little Emma and one of series 110-119, also new in 1900 and top covered in either 1907 or 1908. The building looking slightly reminiscent of a liquorice allsort on the left is The Arcade, designed by Liverpool-born architect Walter Aubrey Thomas (and one of the few premises along here to survive the Second World War). One of the shops within it is a Lyons tea house, part of a chain of cafes started in 1894; up to the last war the rule was waitress service.

Below: Another view of Lord Street shows 207 just leaving the Castle Street junctions. It came from the original large batch of Preston cars delivered in 1900. These were all converted to top-covered in 1903-05. The car is just leaving a stop, indicated by a cast iron sign fixed to the overhead support at about top deck level. The advertisement on the tram was for Nixey's Black Lead, the household staple used to provide a sheen to cast iron firegrates and stoves. The firm was already active in the 1860s and was certainly still trading in the 1920s. They also produced knife polish.

The main municipal buildings were all near Castle Street where the Town Hall is proudly flying the union jack. 342, the first of another 100 Preston cars (still open top then), was delivered in late 1900. The rest came in slightly over a year. This means that ERTC shipped 300 trams in less than two years, an amazing achievement by modern standards. By comparison, Manchester Metrolink received 50 of its new light rail vehicles from the supplier, Bombardier, between 13th July 2009 and 10th March 2012, not far short of three years. Of course, this is comparing chalk with cheese as a modern tram is larger and much more sophisticated than a wooden two axle car, but even so, the achievement of both Dick, Kerr and Liverpool Corporation was very impressive.

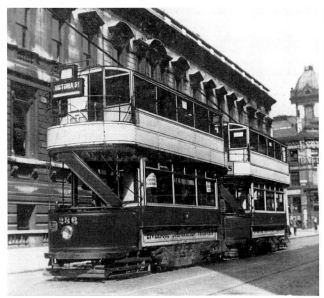

Victoria Street had been driven through an area of slum and back street industry in the late 1860s. It led to Old Haymarket and, in tramway terms, was intended purely as an additional turn-back facility in the city centre as there was only a one-way junction from Lord Street leading to a short section of single track. Bellamy 286 is not showing a route number and is on a football special. It is standing outside Government Buildings, later totally destroyed in an air raid. The site was a car park for decades but has now been utilised for a new museum. 447 is displaying 'Football' on its blind as well as a window poster and is headed for the Liverpool F.C. ground. When the specials reached their destination there was a substantial siding in Priory Road, near the Everton ground, and a shorter one in Walton Breck Road, conveniently placed for Anfield; Walton Depot probably provided a useful storage facility too. 447 was one of 25 open top cars fitted with covers made by Dick, Kerr in 1903, a move designed to speed up the conversion programme. The building beside it did not survive the war but the red brick one beyond it, including the Jerome and Carlisle Buildings, did.

This shows two of the Three Graces, the Royal Liver Friendly Society's head office on the left (built 1908-11) and the Docks Board offices on the right (built 1904-07). The site they were constructed on was the former George's Dock, the wall of which survives to form the river frontage. Opened in 1771, after closure in 1900 it was filled in to provide space for these impressive buildings. The Corporation had initially planned to use the remaining space, partially for new tramway offices, but it was later filled by the Cunard Building (built 1913-16). There are relics here of the area's former dockland status. One plot is owned by the Rochdale Canal Company, whose boats could have accessed this point via the Leeds & Liverpool Canal and the North Docks. In the background is a block of warehouses.

In 1913-14 the tramways took several important steps forward, one of which was the provision of route numbers. Despite the fact that the photographer or copyist has managed to decapitate the tram, this is an important picture. In 1914 several extensions were made. The most significant was the 6A to Broad Green Station (on 27th September 1914) and Bowring Park (on 2nd April 1915). Much of this extension consisted of double track laid off the road, set in lawns and divided from the road by low hedges. The great advantage, of course, was freedom from obstruction for both road and tram traffic. The tram is just coming off the grass track, probably at a road crossing; oddly, the most modern route was served by a rather archaic 'Little Emma' from 1899.

Above: The two main types of car in use towards the end of the first decade of the century were the Straight Staircase class and the Bellamys. A Bellamy leads 'Little Emma' 132 over the junction at Church Street/Lord Street/Whitechapel and Paradise Street. It is a summer's day and the pavements are packed with ladies in fancy hats and gentlemen in their boaters. Headgear said a lot about a person in those days; a workman in his cloth cap is just boarding the rear platform of 132, carefully watched by the conductor from the stairs. The top deck of 132 is lined out in black. The lighter areas were cream, the dark ones red, the red being lined out in gold, the whole forming the standard post-1907 livery; it was all applied by hand, of course.

Overleaf: Two further pictures of 'Little Emmas' with top covers show, first, 68 running along the main road between Bootle and Liverpool. These somewhat dated cars were often allocated to the Bootle/Litherland routes. Stanley Road was crossed here by Strand Road; rebuilding since means that this no longer applies. Most other traffic is horse-drawn, including the smart van on the left belonging to Blackledge's Bakery, a Bootle firm which had shops throughout Liverpool as well. One tends to look at the Edwardian era through rose-tinted spectacles, but the boy pulling the heavy hand cart in the foreground is a reminder of just what a hard working life a working class lad could expect, not to speak of what we would regard as a very early death. In 1900 the average life expectancy for men was only 45 years. 101 is heading out along Lord Street on the Dingle route. Just being passed is a Hansom Cab whilst on the other side two horse carts lumber by. There are a couple more trams in the middle distance, but otherwise 101 has the road to itself.

An electric tram service to Wavertree was first provided on 7th October 1900. On 29th October 1911 First Class cars started via Wavertree to Smithdown Road, but they were withdrawn in 1912-13 because of a coal strike and electricity shortages. Afterwards they were extended to Calderstones on route 4A (a new extension opened on 21st March 1910). Bellamy 563 was built in 1912, very close to the end of the construction period for this type of car and is standing at the Picton Clock, Wavertree, which was presented to the township by Sir James Picton in 1884. He chaired the Liverpool Libraries Committee for nearly 40 years and the fine circular library in the city centre was named after him. Once the centre of a village, today the clock is in the middle of a busy roundabout.

From the 1901 Coronation onwards the tramways marked major events by running the ex-German illuminated tramcar. The city celebrated its 700th anniversary in 1907 with a pageant and several days of festivities. Some standard cars were decorated too and there were two competitions between depot day and night staff to choose which were the best. This is new car 4 from Green Lane's night maintenance crew which won their class. The banner along the side reads "Success to Liverpool" and balanced just below the destination indicator is a rather improbable thatched cottage.

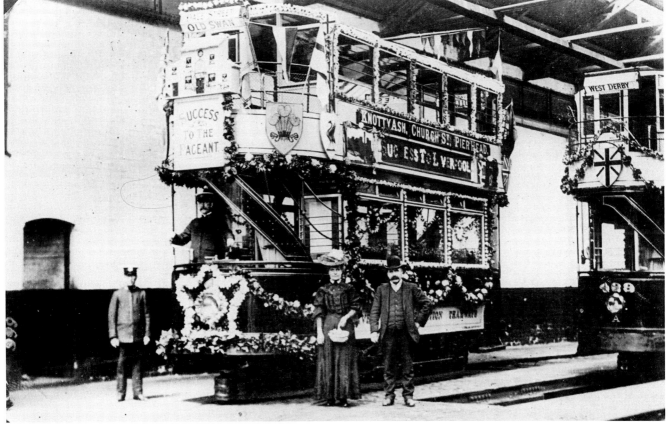

The next major event requiring decorated cars was the Coronation of King George V and Queen Mary in June 1911. 247, a standard Bellamy and not new, was the entry from Smithdown Road. A nearly full-length portrait of the King was placed at one end of the top deck, probably matched by one of the Queen at the other. Two points of tramway interest are the wooden channel covering overhead wiring within depots, required for safety reasons, and – just below the right-hand end of the tram – one of the pits which ran the length of most sidings. They were quite deep, allowing staff to work on items such as motors and brakes from below the tram itself.

Number 250 – illustrated earlier on Dale Street in its open top form – was another Coronation tram. There is lots of bunting and garlands and, round the top deck, a rather nice fabric design which was used on at least one other car and Queen Mary's portrait. It may be a Walton tram as the Aigburth Vale to Aintree route passed near the depot. This was one of the relatively few cross-city tram routes in Liverpool, as most of them ran out and back from the city centre.

No. 255 was also done up for the Coronation, as the 'Empire Car'. Like 247, it had been built in 1900 and retrofitted with a Bellamy cover. The route boards are those used on first class routes but this is only a standard car. The workers photographed in front of it are obviously the men responsible for the elaborate decoration, including the pictures along the side of the top deck, mostly of military personnel. Rather appropriately for Liverpool, though, the ship chosen to illustrate 'One fleet' was not a warship but an ocean liner.

The pre-First World War period was one of enormous disparity of wealth. Unskilled workers were particularly poorly paid and badly housed and they, in reaction, increasingly turned to militant unionism. In 1911 there was a national transport and dock strike, and it was particularly intense in Liverpool. Seamen, dock workers and railwaymen went out and the situation was exacerbated by sectarian strife. By August the tramways had stopped running, mainly due to the power station workers striking. At other times cars were held up by demonstrations and running battles with troops. Here, a line of empty cars is stopped in Lime Street, unable to proceed.

576 was the very last Bellamy tram, though it and 575 differed from all the others in having a top deck roof which included a balcony cover over the ends, following the precedent set by the twin-stair car 571. It was described as a 'Manchester' cover (named after Liverpool's traditional Lancashire rival, the nearest city to use them). Just four Bellamys were built in 1913 and all were painted in white and gold to join the First Class fleet. 576 is pictured sometime after 1920 when a new manager introduced the first roller blind indicators.

576 was constructed in 1913 and around this time a number of other older Bellamy pattern cars were given new roofs with covered balconies. Here 458 and 476 are leaving Victoria Street for Old Haymarket at some time after the Mersey Tunnel had been opened, the elegant lamp standards having been built to highlight the tunnel entrance.

When production ended in 1913 there were 445 Bellamy cars, including 575 and 576. By then most of them were beginning to look dated and, during the First World War, maintenance suffered. Most of the works had been turned over to armaments production, so the trams naturally began to look a bit scruffy. This view of 265 in Tithebarn Street in 1916 certainly shows this. The class, however, still formed the vast bulk of the Liverpool fleet. Realisation of their deficiencies presumably accounted for the third advance (after route numbers and the grass tracks) made in 1912-14, the design of a number of experimental tramcars. The war made large-scale production impossible, but the stage had been set for major improvements once the conflict ended.

C. W. Mallins, the general manager up to and throughout the First World War, had some rather unconventional ideas about how to update the fleet. First of all, a total of seventeen cars with double staircases were built between 1912 (when 571 came out) and 1920, the thought being to provide separate entrances and exits to speed up loading. Cars 583 and 584, pictured, were completed in 1914. All the Double Staircase cars were rather longer than the older ones and experiments were made with radial trucks, the principle being that each pair of wheels was not fixed rigidly but had a limited amount of free movement, so acting more like a bogie and easing the car around curves. The arrangement was not particularly successful anywhere and this example was replaced after only a year. The main feature which was perpetuated was the open-balcony roof. Because 583/4 were particularly long the seating capacity was raised to 80 against 64 on the Bellamy cars. Longer and wider bodywork, however, also meant that the Double Staircase fleet could only be used on certain routes where the trackwork permitted this. They were christened 'Big Emmas' by the staff.

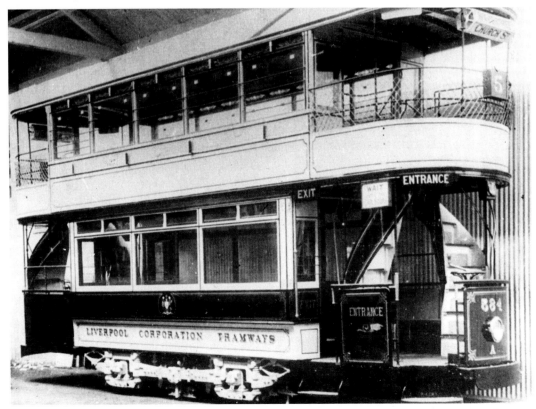

Above and below left: The second experimental type, also built in 1912 by UEC, was a large bogie vehicle with fully enclosed passenger accommodation and a centre entrance. Separate entrance and exit arrangements were again provided, including an 'up' and a 'down' stair. These, looking rather like sets of shelves, are illustrated in the second picture. The lower saloon seats were upholstered in rattan, a type of wicker made from a species of palm. Except for the American single deckers, this was the first bogie tram in Liverpool and had the remarkable total of 83 seats. By the 1930s this sort of design, somewhat modernised, had become fairly popular and was a great crowd mover, but it was not adjudged suitable for Liverpool and 572 remained unique. When Blackpool introduced similar cars in the 1930s it was found necessary to use two conductors or to close off the top deck which, of course, cancelled out most of the economies of scale.

Above right: This is the centre-entrance car in service in 1913. The tram looks massive in its city centre setting. It was not much good on hills, of which Liverpool has plenty and suffered the common fate of many non-standard vehicles of being withdrawn early. It may not have run much or even at all after 1920 and was broken up at the end of the decade. For some reason photographs of Whitechapel are not common, perhaps because its rather less imposing buildings did not attract postcard publishers like Lord Street did. The shop behind the tram is having a 'bargain week'. Sales are not a new invention! It looks distinctly as if the motor car has been parked carelessly and is holding up the tram service, a problem that would get worse.

The final 'one-off' was the least adventurous and, perhaps for that reason, most resembled the design produced in numbers after the First World War. 44 replaced one of the old Westinghouse cars. The main differences from the Bellamys were the covered balcony roof, direct stairs (like the 'Little Emmas'), and the provision of small opening windows upstairs as well as down. It was better than what Liverpool had by then, but still conservative. For some reason it was known as the Exhibition Car, though it was never shown as such. It entered service without fanfare in October 1914, over two months after war had broken out. It is pictured passing the Wellington Column at the corner of William Brown Street and Lime Street about 1930.

This busy scene at the intersection of Lord Street, Whitechapel and Church Street may date from the First World War or immediately afterwards. Both men's and women's fashion is less opulent and women's clothing is more practical with dresses ending above the ankle. During the war, except for a couple of the experimental cars, no new trams could be built either at Lambeth Road or by the established manufacturers, so the service was run largely by the Bellamy cars. They, together with the track and overhead, were in a very poor condition by the time peace came in 1918. A quarter of the fleet was out of service awaiting repair.

Because of the war the delivery of the last twin-staircase car was not made until 1920. The last few appeared with only one stair and the others were all altered to match by 1923. The first and rather indistinct photograph shows 590 in service, probably in its single-staircase form. In 1923 car 588, pictured below in Old Haymarket, had the top deck balconies enclosed too, an improvement later made to the rest of the series. After this design by-way, the efforts of the post-war management were focused on three areas – the development of new but more conservative trams, improvements to the layout of the tracks in the city centre, and expansion of the tramways to serve new suburbs, wherever possible using off-street reserved tracks.

Above: During the war the tramway works had been turned over to munitions manufacture, one reason for the dire post-war shortage of trams. Using the available fleet more efficiently may have been one reason for abandoning all the First Class services in 1923. 542 was a former First Class car seen here after it had been re-liveried into the standard paint scheme. It is running on route 9 to Old Swan via Kensington and is on Church Street. Swears & Wells was a small Liverpool-based chain selling furs and leather clothing; the shop was still there in 1953. Just peering round the corner is one of the more modern trams introduced during the 1920s.

Below: The immediate response to the car shortage was to order 100 new trams from an outside builder, the successors to Dick, Kerr and ERTCW. In the event, only 25 were supplied during 1919 and 1920 and they became known as the English Electric Balcony cars. They were not that different from the last two Bellamys of 1913 or to the Exhibition car. The post-war economic problems did not make this a period when radical change could be contemplated. Car 620 is on route 14 to Carr Lane via Townsend Avenue. As well as new suburban extensions, improvements were made to the city centre layout, including the doubling of tracks along Ranelagh Street, Parker Street and Elliot Street. This picture of Ranelagh Street was taken on 6th September 1932.

Another view of an EE Balcony car, perhaps 623, in Lime Street in the 1920s. None of the cars was ever fully or partially enclosed and some ran unaltered until after the Second World War. The first Adelphi Hotel here dated from 1826, another from 1876, and this final one was built to the instructions of the Midland Railway in luxurious Edwardian style just before the First World War (though not completed till afterwards). It was regarded as the finest hotel outside London. The Sefton Suite is modelled on the first class smoking room of an Atlantic liner; perhaps with hindsight the management might not have chosen the *Titanic*! though it is doubtless good for business today.

This *is* 623, at Pier Head, waiting before making another journey on route 44 to Walton Hall Avenue via Everton and Scotland Road. The crew are taking their layover sitting on the step. Hanging over the dash is an oilskin, needed by the driver on his exposed platform if it rained. To the left of the fleet number is a transfer applied to all cars from the 1920s onwards. It read "SAFETY FIRST. Be sure the road is clear before passing behind this car." The other uniformed man standing to the right of the tram may be a tramway inspector, usually encountered by passengers when checking tickets, but at an important terminus like this they also had the task of ensuring that each car departed on schedule.

An improvement made to the older trams from 1920 was the provision of roller blind indicators instead of the hexagonal slide boxes. This picture was taken during the changeover period as 258 at the front and the rear car have blinds whilst the centre one still has the old slides. Rather ironically, the stencilled route number 5 is much easier to see than the new blind. The trams are on route 5 to Smithdown Rd, Penny Lane and the scene is, of course, Pier Head.

There is quite a line-up of football cars in this view of Victoria Street. It was usual to employ the oldest trams in a fleet for duties such as this and the Bellamys were becoming somewhat dated by the 1930s when this view was probably taken. The slightly more modern car sandwiched between them is one of the EE Balcony trams, recognisable by the very narrow line of ventilators above the upper deck windows. In those days municipalities often provided not only transport but all or most of the utilities as well. Liverpool generated electricity and made gas (from coal) and it was an oddity that, during nearly all the periods when the trams carried advertisements, they proclaimed the virtues of gas rather than electricity.

The Liverpool works produced 34 similar trams in 1920-22. Once again a manager, Percy Priestly, gave his name to these new Standard vehicles. Some were completely new, some incorporated the bodies of old cars, and still more re-used only a few parts of their predecessors; the connection was often very tenuous but the old fleet numbers were retained. 138 was one of one of these 'rebuilds' and is at Carr Lane on 13th September 1928, the terminus for route 43A via Utting Avenue. Both this line and the alternative route via Townsend Avenue were partly on grass tracks, like the pioneer wartime line to Bowring Park, and had opened on 30th July 1924.

This scene outside the Liver Building provides two nice contrasts. The Bellamy looks open and windswept and somehow unfinished. 134 wouldn't be a great improvement on a windy day but at least there was a bit more in the way of rain protection. There is a social contrast in this lively picture too. A smartly-dressed girl follows two or three boys wearing their school caps off the left-hand tram. They are watched by a line of urchins without the benefit of regulation headgear, whilst passing in the foreground is another boy who doesn't even have any socks. Liverpool was (and is today) a city where being a 'have' or a 'have not' starts at an early age (as it does in most urban areas of course). The Priestly car is on route 22A to Aintree.

A Bellamy passes a Priestly Balcony car on Derby Square, the crossing point between Castle Street, South Castle Street, Lord Street and James Street. St. George's Crescent stands as an elegant backdrop, sadly totally destroyed later by wartime bombing. Austin Reed had opened their first store on Fenchurch Street, London in 1900 and offered both tailoring and ready-to-wear suits. There is still a branch in Liverpool. The leading tram is on route 1 Pier Head to Garston via Park Road.

Old Haymarket, next to St. John's Gardens, had been provided with an elaborate set of junctions and crossovers in 1908 to make it suitable as a supplementary terminus. However it was probably too far short of the shopping centre to be very attractive to passengers and it did not see much use. This 1928 view shows some of the 1908 layout. In the following year a lot of the property in the area was demolished in connection with the Mersey Tunnel works and the tram tracks were thinned down. The block on the left includes, in part of the upper floors, the Commercial Temperance Hotel. If this is No. 18 then at one time the 'licensee' was William Hughes. Many such establishments were opened during the 19th and early 20th century and must have attracted enough customers to make them paying ventures.

The next stage in the Priestly Standard's evolution was the provision of closed balconies. The first car to be ready for service was 358, in March, seen here in an official portrait. An immediately obvious difference from the Bellamy type was the tray lifeguard (the earlier Balcony cars had them also). If any object hit the the three-barred 'gate' at the front a tray behind it dropped and would scoop up the object or person. The older cars had all had plough lifeguards, which simply knocked people away from the wheels. There is no particular evidence that the newer ones were any better, but they were fitted to all new Liverpool cars thereafter and retrofitted to many others.

This 1920s scene at Pier Head contrasts the Priestly car with Bellamy 523 in front of it. Each has an open driving position. A disadvantage of the once-preferred reversed stair is that the driver's view to the left could be obscured. The drivers of a restored New Zealand tram were still complaining about this in 2010! The newer car's improved upstairs accommodation included a 'half-horseshoe' bench around one side of the balcony; there is a man sitting on this, facing into the car. Number and route indicators used for this type of car were white on black roller blinds which gave more-or-less total flexibility to use the car anywhere on the system, as opposed to the more limited slide boxes.

Bellamy 258 precedes a semi-enclosed Priestly along Byrom Street, which led into William Brown Street (right) and Dale Street (left). On the right is the Liverpool Technical College (ground floor) and Museum Extension (upper floor), completed in 1901 as the last addition to the William Brown Street range; the World Museum now occupies the entire building. The original entrance was on this side. On the left is Unity House, the city store of the Liverpool Co-operative Society, closed by the early 1960s. The Byrom Street tracks led out to Scotland Road and towards such destinations as Aintree, Fazakerley and Litherland. The date is perhaps the late 1920s or early 1930s.

Another of the semi-enclosed cars stands at Pier Head. It is one of the 120 of this (and the later) design of Standard trams (as the Priestlys will usually be called from now on) built new as opposed to the 201 cars which were regarded as reconstructed; the same 'health warning' applies as with earlier so-called rebuilds. Indeed, the same thing could be said for many old trams which were not, officially, rebuilt. In Liverpool bits were added to bodies, motors were exchanged for more powerful ones, trucks were changed and controllers replaced, leaving little of the original. This tram is an 8 or an 8A travelling to Allerton via Mather Avenue. To the left of it is one of the 'floating' bridges leading from dry land to the Landing Stage.

Church Street is full of the more modern type of tram in this view, probably taken in the mid-1920s, and giving a much more up-to-date image of the city's tramway undertaking. Just about the only other form of transport on the streets is provided by motor taxis. The white building in the centre background was erected on the site of St. Peter's Church in 1922-3 by Woolworths. The block was larger than they needed so other parts of it were rented to other retailers, including C&A Modes and Montague Burtons, the Leeds-based tailors. The building is still there and forms part of the Liverpool One retail development. Burtons is still in the same shop on the far corner.

It was, however, still possible to find scenes on the tramway which did not seem to have changed much since well before the First World War. A Standard Balcony car is just on its way down Lime Street, but the other three trams are all Bellamys. The car drawn up against the kerb is a Morris Bullnose, a design first built in 1913-14 and again in 1919-1926. However there is a marked absence of traffic and pedestrians are able to wander anywhere at will. The track in the foreground is the (at the time, still) single line bringing trams up from Church Street.

This photograph of the Pier Head is taken from a rather unconventional viewpoint. It shows Bellamy 377 on route 16 to Litherland. It is still using the pre-war destination indicator system rather than the newer roller blinds. Beside it is a line of taxis, their high bodies possibly being based on the Austin 12/4 chassis; if so, these were introduced from 1928 onwards. Above the portico of the Liver Building one can read the word 'society' for the full title of the owners at the time was The Royal Liver Friendly Society. It had been founded in 1850 as the Lyver Burial Society, a simple form of insurance to cover an obvious need, and – before a recent amalgamation – was later known as Royal Liver Assurance, still a mutual rather than a commercial company.

Between 1926 and 1935 the late evening trams on many but not all routes provided a postal collection service, using these special post boxes hanging on the dash. This is a 'staged' view at Garston Terminus as normally it would have been dark when postal cars were running. The woman in the shawl is typical of how many women would have dressed at the time. 130 is one of the latest pattern of semi-enclosed cars.

Both open and closed balcony types are seen together with many older Bellamy-roofed trams on Warbreck Moor, Aintree, in the 1920s. There are other meetings at the race course and the Grand National event itself takes place over three days, but it is the eponymous race itself which really draws the crowds, seen here streaming off the trams (and trains) towards the course. The photographer is standing on the L&Y or (from 1923) London, Midland & Scottish Railway (LMS) overbridge near the special station, only used for race day excursions.

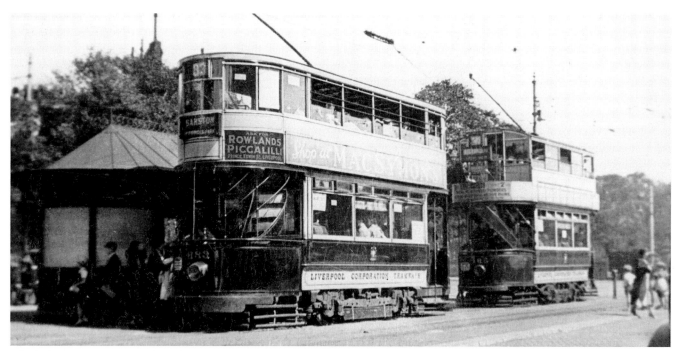

The first post-war move of lines from the street to reservation was in 1922 along Princes Road. It involved shifting the existing street track in one of the parallel carriageways across to form a gravelled reservation along one side of the trees in the centre of the boulevard. The photograph shows 683, a Priestly Standard car new in November 1925. Some contrasts with Bellamy 165, behind, are the direct stairs, the balconies of course, and the absence of advertisement panels on the front of the car. 683 was a completely new tram and though more than half the class were theoretically rebuilds, all had new bodies, and if the motors were not refitted took over only a few minor parts (plus, once again, the numbers).

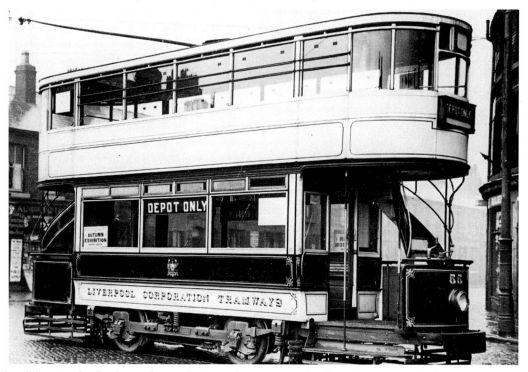

The body style of the Standards changed over the years but many technological experiments and improvements took place as well. The first trucks had a 7 feet 6 inches wheelbase but this was fairly soon lengthened to 8 feet 6 inches. In the beginning they were supplied by Brill but later the works began constructing their own. Car 55, pictured, used a new design by Brill, the 79E2, but it was the same length. The newly-built car illustrates how smart the trams looked in their dark red and cream livery when no external advertisements had been applied; there are just some posters in the windows advertising an 'Autumn exhibition'. It is perhaps outside Walton Depot, the largest in the city.

Castle Street, as its name implies, was one of the original streets of the medieval borough. It frames the splendid Town Hall, the third (or by some definitions the fourth) on the site. Part of John Wood the Younger's building of 1754 is incorporated within it, but it was severely damaged by fire in 1795. James Wyatt then designed a new one with a much larger central dome and adding the Corinthian portico. Finally, it was extended in 1811. The postcard photographer probably took this view in 1932. It shows how Bellamy cars were still running in daily service then. This one is going to Croxteth Road via Myrtle Street. Behind it a Standard car with enclosed balcony is just turning into Water Street on the way to Pier Head.

This next view is probably slightly earlier and shows the crossroads between James Street, on the left, Lord Street, on the right, and Castle and South Castle Streets. The complex trackwork allowed trams to move in almost any direction. Naturally the overhead linesmen had to follow the tracks with their complex skeins of overhead wiring. The live wires were those immediately over the track, like the curve to the right. The cross wires were known as span wires and their function was only to provide support – so they were 'dead'. After the Edwardian period, it was usual to find this method of construction in the city centre, with the span wires attached to buildings by so-called 'rosettes'.

Apart from anything else, these two views of Pier Head taken on 24th July 1931 are a reminder that Liverpool is a maritime city, with Atlantic gales bringing plenty of wet weather in their wake. About ten years before, an important remodelling of this major city terminus had taken place so that, in place of the former two loops, there were now three. The overhead wiring was especially complex here and – in the absence of convenient buildings – was largely supported on strategically placed poles. The first picture shows two Bellamys and one of the Priestly Standards already described. The second has, in the background, an example of the next stage in the evolution of these vehicles, a weatherproof driver's position. The driver of this particular car must have been very grateful on this dreadful summer's day.

Priestly himself had a somewhat old-fashioned view on this issue of drivers' windscreens and considered that the men would be better in the open. However, he was overruled by the Tramways Committee, and in 1927 the first fully-enclosed tram, 742, appeared. Since no-one in the works quite knew how to do this, many panes of glass of assorted sizes were employed, giving the car the soubriquet of 'Crystal Palace'. Other experiments were made and a simplified design was used after that.

In the picture below more or less the final version of the fully-enclosed Standard type is represented by 88, waiting at the pier head. The eventual design for the front vestibule was much less 'home-made' looking, giving the whole car a neat and pleasing appearance. On a warm day, as this must have been, ventilation was provided for lower deck passengers by a line of small opening windows, known as quarter lights, above the large panes. These were angled to act as scoops to draw in fresh air. As can be seen, the upper deck windows along the sides could be lowered almost to their full depth; external rails were provided for safety.

Above: A semi-enclosed Priestly Standard is standing on one of the Pier Head loops with its windows open. The car behind is probably an EE Balcony type. A crowd of passengers is waiting for their tram, including someone who has left their luggage on the pavement, probably having just arrived on the ferry. In the background is the Mersey Docks & Harbour Board building.

Below: Another view at the Princes Road shelter shows the differences between the semi- and fully-enclosed models with car 106 on the left and 26 on the right. There was an intensive tram service over several routes along here; in this picture cars on lines 15 and 25 are standing at the stop.

These two views represent Priestly's achievement. In each case, one Bellamy tram is outnumbered by trams designed to the manager's specifications. The first photograph shows Water Street, with the Town Hall at the rear on the left and Pier Head behind the photographer. In this case there is a mixture of semi- and fully-enclosed cars. The tracks to the left here took cars across to St. Nicholas Place to reach the north terminal loop. In the second view, at Pier Head itself, all the trams (except the sole Bellamy) are fully enclosed and they represent what was, for many British tramways, the limit of their evolution. 336 looks smart and well turned out and, with its capacity of around 70 seated and standing passengers would have been a good crowd mover.

Car 746 came towards the end of the Priestly programme and had certain non-standard features. It was one of 25 cars with 20 feet bodies as against the normal 16 feet 6 inches and these longer trams all used radial trucks, the idea being to mimic the action of bogies without going to the expense of the extra equipment. In 1927 when drivers' windows were being considered 746 (and 745) briefly received an experimental partial screen. Route 1 ran between Pier Head and Garston. This is, of course, Bunney's corner but from a different direction. Horne Brothers was a fairly high class tailoring concern based in Hackney. The chain went into liquidation in 2012.

Another view of the Pier Head taken on 24th July 1931 is much more typical of the balance within the tram fleet. Car 620, on the left, is one of the EE Balcony series and, so, probably, is the one on the extreme right. In between them is sandwiched a Bellamy car and behind that is a fully-enclosed Standard type. A feature of the Pier Head terminus at this period was the large destination displays built on to some of the overhead poles.

Bellamy 272 stands there a little earlier. The panels on the stop sign were made of glass and – presumably – illuminated at night; they gave very clear guidance to intending passengers. The Bellamy car has been retrofitted with roller-blind indicators which include a route number, destination and via box. The latter was probably often slightly inaccurate in one direction of the travel. In this case it is correct for inward bound but outward bound cars would run along Water Street before arriving at Dale Street. 'Briskies' were a rival to the American Kelloggs. According to people's memories they were not very tasty!

This is the North Loop. Cars on some of the services listed are waiting to depart, the one on the right on route 17 to Seaforth and that nearest the camera via route 44 to Walton Hall Avenue along Everton Valley and Scotland Road. Smoke rises from some industrial or dock premises in the background. Liverpool between the wars was very much a working city. In these days the number of building societies has been drastically trimmed by, most recently, the 2008 financial crisis, but earlier a large city would have not one but several. The Liverpool Benefit Society's head office was in India Buildings, Water Street, so-called because the original edifice was named to commemorate the ending of the East India Company's monopoly on trade to that country. A replacement block was completed in 1932.

There were three combinations of streets by which trams entered or left the Pier Head terminus, St. Nicholas Place/Chapel Street/Water Street, Water Street itself and Mann Island/James Street. St. Nicholas Place (really a part of Pier Head itself) was a common subject of Edwardian postcards but for some reason most later photographers seemed to choose to confine themselves to Water Street. These are day and night views of semi-enclosed cars passing underneath the Elevated Railway viaduct. Both were taken on 24th July 1931, clearly a long day out for the photographer! The first shows car 32 and the second 666. The wildly varying fleet numbers were not, of course, due to there being well over 600 cars of that type but to the fact that just over 100 Priestlys were new and the remainder were officially rebuilds of much earlier trams. Persons of a religious nature ought not have ventured on No. 666, especially in the dark, for this is the famous mark of the beast from the book of Revelation! It is a wonderfully atmospheric view though.

WATER STREET, LIVERPOOL. 217/71.J.Y.

A varied collection of old and new trams is seen in this postcard view of Water Street. There are a couple of enclosed Standards, a pair of Bellamys and, at the back, a semi-enclosed Standard. The leading Bellamy is turning out of Castle Street and on the right is the imposing portico of the Town Hall. The impressive office block behind it is the head office of Martins Bank, built 1927-32 to the design of H. J. Rowse, an architect who was also closely involved with the Mersey Tunnel. Martins resulted from a merger in 1918 between the institution of that name and the Bank of Liverpool and it became one of the few major English financial concerns to be headquartered outside London (the Halifax Building Society was another). In 1969 it was sold to Barclays.

ST. GEORGE'S HALL AND LIME STREET, LIVERPOOL.

Above: This postcard again demonstrates how in the 1920s the fleet was quite a mixture of elderly, improved and – by the standards of the day – modern trams. The enclosed Standard standing on the terminal track in the centre is on route 28 which ran from here to Litherland. Motor cars are parked on the area to the left and passing are a number of taxis, both competitors to the trams (though the size and opulence of most of the cars means that only the wealthiest had one). A more serious threat was posed by the motor bus. One, parked just below St. George's Hall, is an Albion Motors Valkyrie vehicle owned by McShanes Services Ltd. This operator ran routes to Bootle under contentious circumstances only in 1932-33, but there were several other more significant firms.

Below: The two largest bus concerns were Crosville and Ribble. Until 1931 local authorities had powers to license bus routes and major tramway operators, like Liverpool, used that to restrict competition by refusing to allow company buses to pick up along tram routes or exiling their vehicles to out of the way terminals. After 1931 independent traffic commissioners took over and the city had then to come to an agreement with the two groups. Three areas were delineated, zone A (Corporation monopoly), zone B (costs and revenue of company and Corporation operations shared), and zone C (company-only). None of this affected any tramway in the outer zones, except by competition. So, in the background of this picture of Bellamy 231 at the Pier Head south loop, the Ribble bus now has a central terminus.

The recovery of the tramways from their 1918 nadir involved other important developments as well as fleet renewal. Related to the latter, though, was the building of completely new workshop premises at Edge Lane to replace Lambeth Road, which had been developed piecemeal and was very cramped. Edge Lane was purpose-built on a very spacious site. It was erected between 1924 and 1928 and next to it was a new tram depot. Modern machinery provided all the necessary facilities for maintaining the fleet and building more-or-less complete new trams. This pre-opening scene demonstrates how the overhead cranes could lift car bodies off their trucks. Priestly *747* was a non-standard version with a longer body than normal.

A further important change was the improvement of the track layout in the city centre. For example, in 1929-30 the single lines in Parker Street and Ranelagh Street were both doubled which meant that tram traffic could flow more freely. This postcard of Parker Street must date from almost this time as most of the trams in the street are old-fashioned Bellamy cars; later in the decade they began to disappear quite rapidly. The corner of the bigger building was occupied by Reece's, who had a bakery on the ground floor, a restaurant on the second, and a dance floor above that where young ladies would go for tea dances. Both the large blocks are still there today, Reece's corner being occupied by Superdrug. The street itself is pedestrianised.

Ranelagh Street & Adelphi, Liverpool. 6765.

This shows the double tracks in Ranelagh Street outside Central Station. The Bellamy car is on route 45 from Dingle (Mill Street) to Pier Head via Great George Street. The building in the far background is the opulent Adelphi Hotel. Facing it on Lime Street is Lewis's department store, at one time probably the most well-known shop in the city. It was founded in 1856 and branches were later opened in other cities, but entered liquidation in 1991. The Liverpool shop continued trading under different ownerships but finally closed in 2010, as much as anything a victim of the shift in shopping patterns caused by retail developments elsewhere in the city centre.

These photographs again illustrate the new double lines in Ranelagh Street. Taken at the same stop, they show the contrast between two trams designed a quarter century apart. 272 dated from 1900 and 459 came from the series built (and often later improved) over the 1920s and early 1930s. Routes 5 and 15 ran to the same quadrant of the city, the former to Penny Lane and the latter to Croxteth Road. The tall block just behind the tram was occupied by Charles & Co who were, amongst other things, clockmakers. The corner of Lewis' store is just visible on the right and the Adelphi Hotel, on Lime Street, is again in the background.

The final key change was the building of miles of new lines into the developing suburbs. This process had already begun before 1914 and this spacious track along Menlove Avenue had initially been opened on 21st March 1910, together with three other new extensions. It was used by First Class route 4A to Calderstones. Bellamy 523 was turned out from Lambeth Road in the same year. It is pictured on 3rd June 1920 as, surprisingly, the cream cars ran throughout the First World War until 5th April 1923. A change in the social composition of the city was another reason for having 'one class' travel. On 19th July 1924 this line was extended to Woolton, this time using the grass track type of construction pioneered to Bowring Park in 1914. Semi-enclosed Priestley 645 is pictured on Menlove Avenue in July around the time when the new extension was opened. The type of construction involved a base of clinker and wooden sleepers, on which the rails were laid, then infilled with soil and seeded with grass. It was much cheaper than street track and separated trams and other road vehicles. Neat privet hedges completed the effect. The lack of housing was typical; these were lines designed to create traffic rather than to serve existing demand.

Further out along route 5A to Woolton, semi-enclosed Standard 645 is pictured at Woolton High Street shortly after the new line had opened. Just as in the previous view, the hedges are still rather spindly. Bollards were placed at the ends of reserved track sections to make reasonably sure that road traffic did not enter them, though probably on dark or foggy nights the odd mistake did occur. Much earlier, in 1902, a straggling single track tramway had been opened between Knotty Ash and Prescot, on the outskirts of St. Helens. This was a private company's venture but when, in 1919, they wished to sell up, Liverpool bought the line and converted it to grass track standards in 1921-23.

A further connection between Liverpool and its hinterland was the East Lancashire Road, opened in 1934, and the first purpose-built inter-city highway in the UK. The idea stemmed from the 1920s and, in the same decade, the city gained parliamentary powers for two other major road projects, the Mersey Tunnel and the Everton Tunnel, the latter being part of a plan to connect the river crossing with the trunk road. It was initially intended that both tunnels would include tramways, for which single deck trams would have been required. So, in 1928, a sample car was purchased from English Electric. The body was largely 'off the shelf', being similar to the contemporary Blackpool Pullman cars. 757 was photographed on test at Preston prior to delivery. The trolley pole is a fake, having been painted in.

This is a contemporary postcard of the first Mersey Tunnel, which was opened by King George V on 18th July 1934 (the same day as the official opening of the East Lancs Road). It ran between Liverpool and Birkenhead and has a branch tunnel at each end to serve the docks. The actual bore is circular and the tram tracks – if constructed – would have run below the road decking. The space was instead used for a gas pipe (now out of service) but is still essential for ventilation purposes. Had the tramways of Liverpool, Birkenhead and Wallasey been connected in this way the whole subsequent history of tram transport in the area might have been very different.

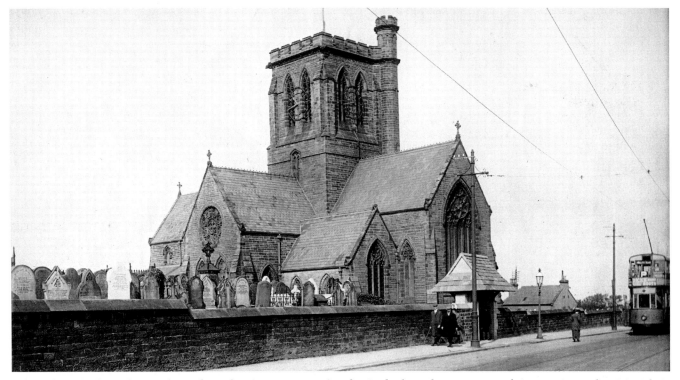

When the tunnel was being planned, neither 'cross-Mersey' authority had any longer got much interest in modernising their tramways. The Wallasey tram system remained stuck in a time warp with a large fleet of Bellamy-style cars and, though they did provide some vestibules, the balconies remained open. All four tram routes ran, literally, from A to B (or Seacombe to New Brighton), but by different roads. Route P passed Harrison Drive. This car is beside St. Hilary's Church, reconstructed and reopened in 1857 following a disastrous fire. There has been a church on the site for at least 1,500 years. The last trams were replaced by buses in 1933, the year before the Mersey Tunnel opened.

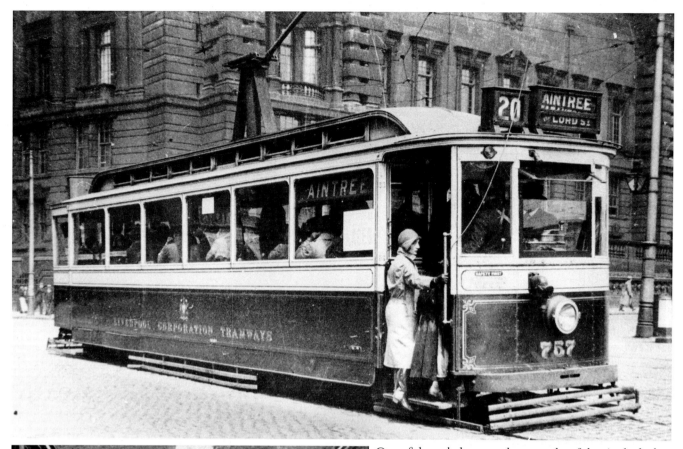

One of the only known photographs of the single decker (sometimes known as the 'tunnel car') in service, in Old Haymarket, in July 1932. The poster in the window advertises transport to the races via route 20 to Aintree. *757* was of course a bogie car and Percy Priestly and English Electric designed some technical improvements to the drive mechanism from the motors to the wheels. These worked well enough but were not entirely successful. It had been intended to run the car with a trailer, but that was never built.

This is the saloon of the car in a view taken in 1929. There were two rows of comfortably-upholstered seats and, a luxurious touch, lamp shades. Passengers were impressed and drivers liked driving the modern car. However the long narrow gangway and the rather cramped platforms made it slow to load and unload, meaning that, despite a good turn of speed, it was hard to keep to time. Partly as a result, *757* was withdrawn in 1934 and scrapped the following year.

The next step, in 1931-33, was to produce eleven double-deck bogie trams, 759-769. The bodies were built locally but English Electric supplied sets of similar bogies to the 'tunnel' car plus control gear. Each bogie had one motor driving both wheels, which gave greater adhesion whilst still saving by having only one motor instead of two. Normal hand-operated controllers were fitted to most cars but soon replaced by the new equipment ordered from English Electric. This was a form of remote control operated from a small panel at the driver's position and moving the switchgear by pneumatic action. These two official views show a pair of the new cars outside Edge Lane Works in 1931-2. In the top picture the fairing covering the bogies has been removed to show the modern arrangement of wheels outside the truck frames. Clear side destination and via screens were provided.

This photograph, taken by a tram enthusiast in September 1933, is of 760 in service at Pier Head on route 10A to Knotty Ash. These cars looked very smart in the traditional red and cream livery and, body-wise, were an extended version of the latest fully-enclosed Priestly Standards. The same ventilation arrangements applied as with the older cars, with three-quarter drop upper saloon windows and quarter lights below. Seating capacity was 70 as against around 60 on the later Priestlys.

A final view of footballs specials leaving Victoria Street, again taken by an enthusiast, show how many out-dated cars were still in the fleet even in the early 1930s. This is a slightly unfair impression to leave, as football cars were always operated by older cars. But there were evidently still plenty of Bellamys able to be turned out for such duties. 314 follows a balcony-roofed car. Beside it is an Austin 7; it looks like the 1931 saloon version.

However this view of the Lord Street/North John Street junction, taken in 1934, shows that old trams ran on normal services too. Of the five leading cars, four are Bellamys and just one is a Priestley with an enclosed top. The first is on route 33 from Garston to Pier Head. Queues of trams were probably not that uncommon as a large number were running to or from Pier Head at any one time. To alleviate this, supplementary services were run from other points in the city centre to various outer termini. The building beside car 236 is under repair and houses Woodhouse & Sons, house furnishers, who had premises along Lord Street. The shop was destroyed during the war but the firm was back in business from temporary premises by, at latest, 1948.

The penultimate photograph in this book is taken from almost exactly the same viewpoint as the second and is dominated again by St. George's Hall. The concert hall, the purpose behind its construction, is in the centre, indicated by the large windowless attic. At either end were court buildings; it was as late as 1994 before these became redundant, allowing conversion to other uses. Instead of horse-drawn, it is internal combustion vehicles that are parked at The Lime Street Quadrant, including a lorry, taxis and – from the tramcars' point of view – most threateningly, two half-cab charabancs or buses. The passing tram, on route 29, is a fully-enclosed four-wheel car typical of the stage of development which UK tramways had reached in the 1930s.

Priestly himself died in 1933 after a period of illness. Bellamy car 295, built in 1900 and seen at Dingle around 1930, epitomises some of the problems he left behind him. There were too many old trams. Priestly's own four-wheelers were developed into workmanlike trams, but they were already dated. The bus side of the undertaking was in a mess and major competitive pressure was being felt from private bus companies. The manager had been hampered by that bugbear of municipal enterprise – councillors who thought they were executives. As a result of all this, the financial situation was poor and getting worse. A great majority of small to medium sized tramways had already closed by 1933 and some major ones were showing signs of following. Manchester closed its first route in 1930 and London replaced many of its trams by trolleybuses in the same decade. Tramway closure was in the air. Would Liverpool's survive?

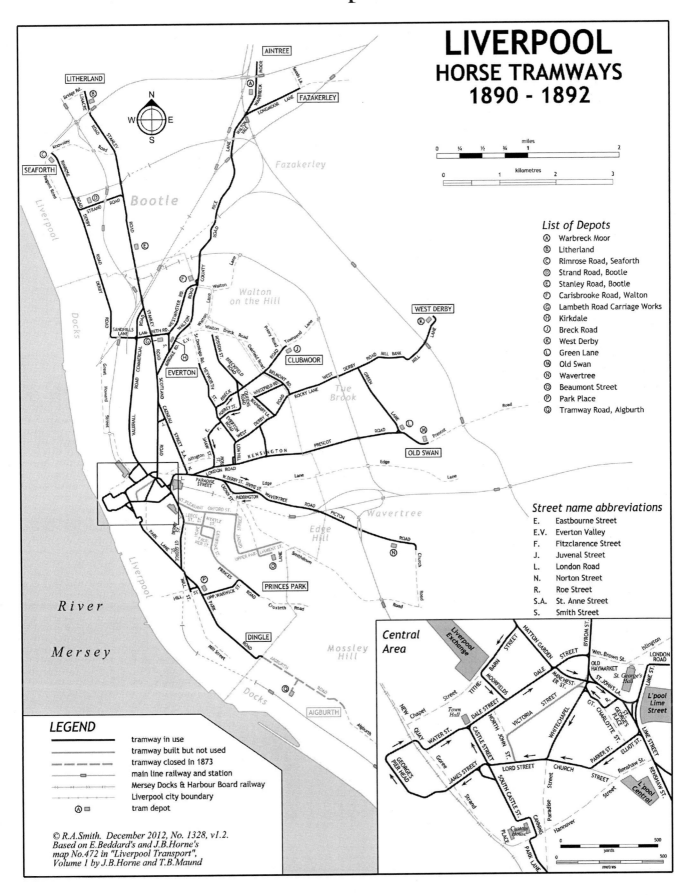

LIVERPOOL
HORSE TRAMWAYS
1890 - 1892

List of Depots

- Ⓐ Warbreck Moor
- Ⓑ Litherland
- Ⓒ Rimrose Road, Seaforth
- Ⓓ Strand Road, Bootle
- Ⓔ Stanley Road, Bootle
- Ⓕ Carisbrooke Road, Walton
- Ⓖ Lambeth Road Carriage Works
- Ⓗ Kirkdale
- Ⓙ Breck Road
- Ⓚ West Derby
- Ⓛ Green Lane
- Ⓜ Old Swan
- Ⓝ Wavertree
- Ⓞ Beaumont Street
- Ⓟ Park Place
- Ⓠ Tramway Road, Aigburth

Street name abbreviations

E.	Eastbourne Street
E.V.	Everton Valley
F.	Fitzclarence Street
J.	Juvenal Street
L.	London Road
N.	Norton Street
R.	Roe Street
S.A.	St. Anne Street
S.	Smith Street

LEGEND

———	tramway in use
═══	tramway built but not used
– – –	tramway closed in 1873
	main line railway and station
	Mersey Docks & Harbour Board railway
	Liverpool city boundary
Ⓐ ▦	tram depot

© R.A.Smith. December 2012, No. 1328, v1.2.
Based on E.Beddard's and J.B.Horne's
map No.472 in "Liverpool Transport",
Volume 1 by J.B.Horne and T.B.Maund

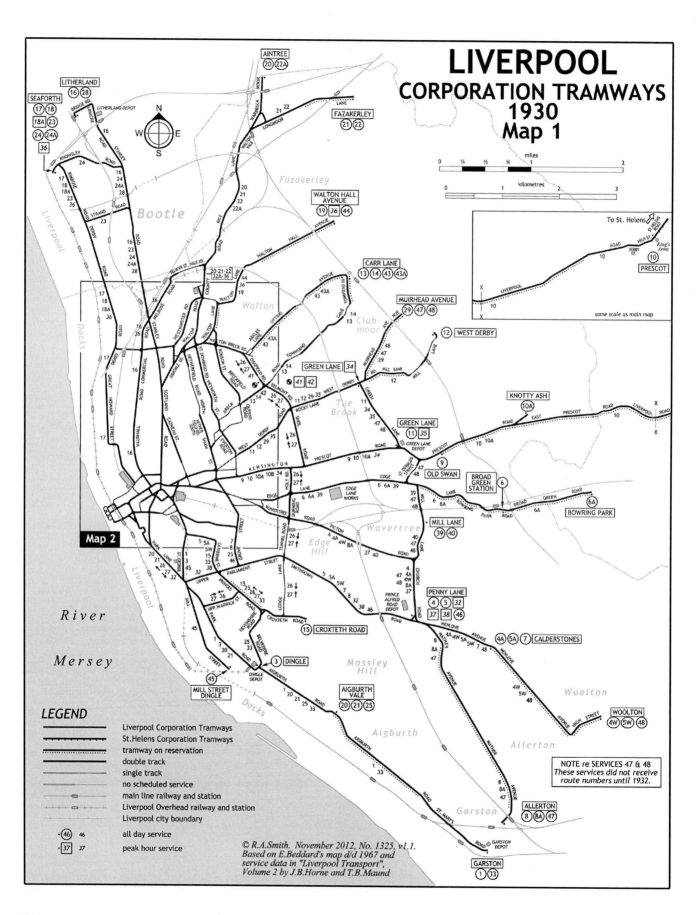

LIVERPOOL
CORPORATION TRAMWAYS
1930
Map 1

LEGEND

————	Liverpool Corporation Tramways
————	St.Helens Corporation Tramways
··········	tramway on reservation
━━━━	double track
————	single track
━━━━	no scheduled service
	main line railway and station
+++++	Liverpool Overhead railway and station
	Liverpool city boundary
(46) 46	all day service
(37) 37	peak hour service

NOTE re SERVICES 47 & 48
These services did not receive
route numbers until 1932.

© R.A.Smith. November 2012, No. 1325, v1.1.
Based on E.Beddard's map d/d 1967 and
service data in "Liverpool Transport",
Volume 2 by J.B.Horne and T.B.Maund

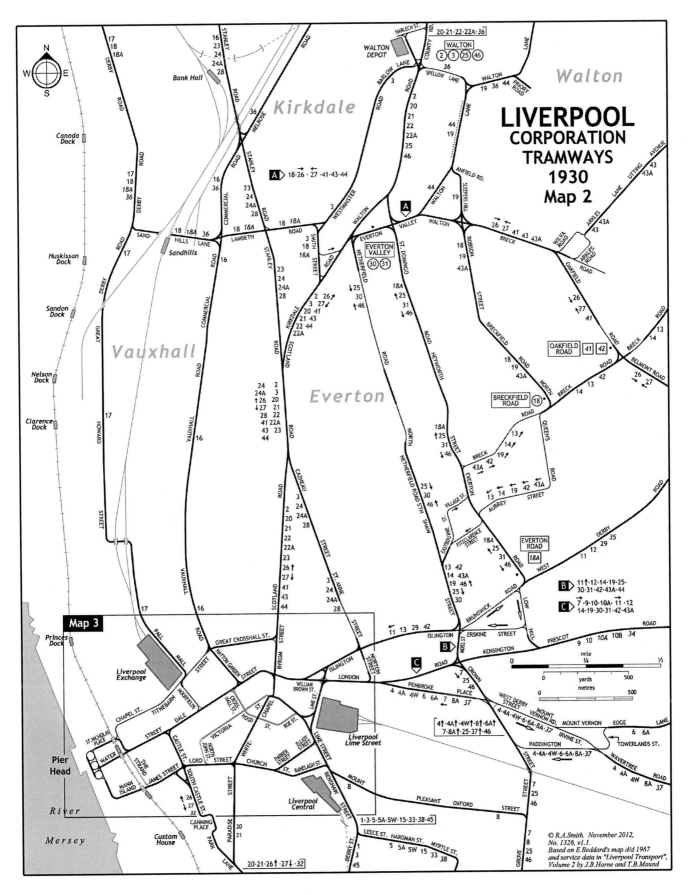

LIVERPOOL CORPORATION TRAMWAYS 1930 Map 2

© R.A.Smith. November 2012,
No. 1326, v1.1.
Based on E.Beddard's map d/d 1967
and service data in "Liverpool Transport",
Volume 2 by J.B.Horne and T.B.Maund

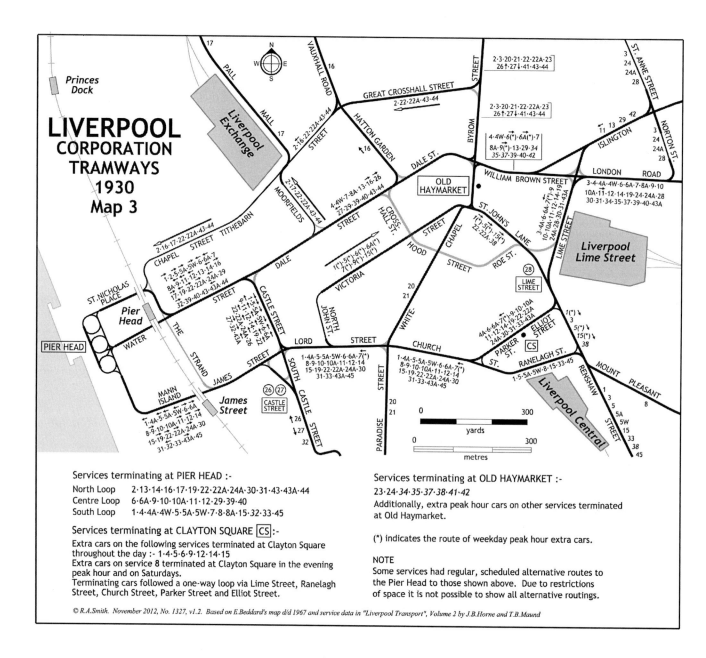

LIVERPOOL CORPORATION TRAMWAYS 1930 Map 3

Princes Dock

Liverpool Exchange

Liverpool Lime Street

Liverpool Central

OLD HAYMARKET

LIME STREET

Pier Head

PIER HEAD

James Street

CASTLE STREET

CS

North Loop 2·13·14·16·17·19·22·22A·24A·30·31·43·43A·44

Services terminating at PIER HEAD :-

North Loop   2·13·14·16·17·19·22·22A·24A·30·31·43·43A·44
Centre Loop   6·6A·9·10·10A·11·12·29·39·40
South Loop   1·4·4A·4W·5·5A·5W·7·8·8A·15·32·33·45

Services terminating at CLAYTON SQUARE CS :-

Extra cars on the following services terminated at Clayton Square
throughout the day :- 1·4·5·6·9·12·14·15
Extra cars on service 8 terminated at Clayton Square in the evening
peak hour and on Saturdays.
Terminating cars followed a one-way loop via Lime Street, Ranelagh
Street, Church Street, Parker Street and Elliot Street.

Services terminating at OLD HAYMARKET :-

23·24·34·35·37·38·41·42

Additionally, extra peak hour cars on other services terminated
at Old Haymarket.

(*) indicates the route of weekday peak hour extra cars.

NOTE

Some services had regular, scheduled alternative routes to
the Pier Head to those shown above. Due to restrictions
of space it is not possible to show all alternative routings.

© R.A.Smith. November 2012, No. 1327, v1.2. Based on E.Beddard's map d/d 1967 and service data in "Liverpool Transport", Volume 2 by J.B.Horne and T.B.Maund

OUTLINE FLEET LIST 1897-1932

1st Nos.	2nd Nos.	Type	Date	Builder	Notes
400 – 414		Altona	1898	Busch	1
401 – 415		Altona	1898	Busch	
416 – 428		Ringbahn	1898	Busch	2
417 – 429		Ringbahn	1898	Busch	3
	1 – 4	Bellamy	1907	LCT	
	5	Single-ended	1901	LCT	4
432 – 446	6 – 20	American	1898	Brill	5
447 – 458	21 – 32	BTH	1899	Milnes	6
459 – 463	43 – 47	Westinghouse	1899	Brush	6
464 – 468		Brush	1899	Brush	7
469 – 478	33 – 42	Straight Stair	1899-1900	ERTC	8
	54 – 133 & 14	Straight Stair	1899-1900	ERTC	9
479 – 484	48 – 53	Lambeth Rd	1899	LCT	10
	134 – 140	Experimental	1899-1902	LCT	11
	142 – 441	Preston	1900-1901	ERTC	12
	442 – 447	Bellamy	1903	LCT	13
	448 – 452	Preston	1902-1903	ERTC	14
	453 – 477	Bellamy	1902-1903	ERTC	13
	478 – 483	Preston	1903	LCT	14
	484 – 500	Bellamy	1907	LCT	
	501 – 519	Bellamy	1908	LCT	15
	520 – 529	Bellamy	1909	LCT	
	530 – 546	Bellamy	1910	LCT	16
	547 – 570	Bellamy	1911-1912	LCT	
	573 – 576	Bellamy	1913	LCT	17
	571	Double Staircase	1913	UEC	
	572	Centre Entrance	1913	UEC	
	577 – 605	Double Staircase	1913-1920	LCT	18
	44 (2)	Exhibition	1914	LCT	19
	609 – 633	EE Balcony	1919-1920	EE	
	606 – 8 / 34 – 36	Priestley Balcony	1920-1922	LCT	20
	637 – 756	Priestley	1924-27	LCT	21

NOTES

1. All German cars small single-deckers; odd numbers were trailers.
2. 428 illuminated car (1902); 418-424 = cash vans LR2 & LR3 (1905); 416 tow car for scrubbers (1906); 422 scrubber (1907).
3. Both classes withdrawn by 1901. 429 tool van till 1950; scrapped 1955 ff. failed preservation attempt.
4. Unsuccessful & quickly converted; number passed to a nominal 'rebuild' in 1929.
5. Single deck, centre entrance; 6, 8 & 12 converted to double deck (1900-1909): all withdrawn by 1926-27.
6. American Peckham Cantilever trucks.
7. Rejected; bought by Leeds.
8. Trial cars prior to bulk order.
9. Nearly all, including trial cars, later top covered; last withdrawn or 'rebuilt' 1928-1929.
10. Bodies of 48-50 sold to Gateshead in 1921; others rebodied until scrapped 1927-9; body of 51 to new illuminated car.
11. Varying styles; 139 became the prototype for mass production.
12. The new standard car, like 139; all Prestons later covered, then being classed as Bellamys or Covered Prestons.
13. Fitted with experimental canvas covers (as were some later cars); all Preston/Bellamy cars provided with more permanent covers by 1905.
14. The last to enter service with open tops.
15. The first delivered with solid top covers; all others retrofitted over several years.
16. 535, 543 & 544 built wide lower saloons & 2/2 seating.
17. 575 & 576 had 'Manchester' type top covers with balcony covers, some cars retro-fitted.
18. 600, 601 & 605 had only a single stair; earlier cars later converted to match.
19. Direct stairs & roofed balconies; similar to post-war Priestly Standards.
20. Some later fully enclosed.
21. Dates given for cars with 'new' numbers; rebuilds, nominal or otherwise, came out 1922-32.

Tramcar Builders

Some of these concerns also supplied trucks, electrical equipment etc.

Ashbury	Ashbury Railway Carriage & Iron Co. Ltd, Manchester
Brill	J.G. Brill Company, Philadelphia, USA
BTH	British Thomson Houston Co. Ltd, Rugby
Brush	Brush Electrical Engineering Co. Ltd, Loughborough
Busch	Waggonfabrik W. C. F. Busch, Hamburg
EE*	English Electric Co. Ltd, Preston
ERTCW*	Electric Railway & Tramway Carriage Works Ltd, Preston
LCT	Liverpool Corporation Tramways (*later* Passenger Transport)
Milnes	Geo F. Milnes & Co. Ltd, Birkenhead (later of Hadley, Shropshire)
Starbuck	George Starbuck & Company, Birkenhead (horse cars only)
UEC	United Electric Car Company Ltd, Preston

Suppliers of Electrical Equipment & Trucks

Dick, Kerr*	Dick, Kerr & Co. Ltd, Preston
Curtis	Curtis Truck Company, Decatur, Illinois, USA
Peckham USA	Peckham Motor Truck & Wheel Company, New York
Peckham UK	Peckham Truck & Engineering Co. Ltd
Schuckert	W. S. Schuckert, Nuremberg
Westinghouse USA	Westinghouse Electric & Manufacturing Company, Pittsburgh
Westinghouse UK	British Westinghouse Electric & Manufacturing Co., Trafford Park

*All associated companies, later trading under the English Electric name.